Henry H. Parker
From his Father
Christmas 1871

AFRICAN FOREST.

MY APINGI KINGDOM:

WITH LIFE IN THE

GREAT SAHARA,

AND SKETCHES OF

THE CHASE OF THE OSTRICH, HYENA, &c.

By PAUL DU CHAILLU,

AUTHOR OF

"DISCOVERIES IN EQUATORIAL AFRICA," "STORIES OF THE GORILLA COUNTRY,'
"ASHANGO LAND," "WILD LIFE UNDER THE EQUATOR," &c.

NUMEROUS ENGRAVINGS.

NEW YORK:
HARPER & BROTHERS, PUBLISHERS,
FRANKLIN SQUARE.
1871.

CONTENTS.

CHAPTER XVIII.

CHAPTER XIX.

CHAPTER XX.

CHAPTER XXI.

CHAPTER XXII.

CHAPTER XXIII.

CHAPTER XXIV.

CHAPTER XXV.

CHAPTER XXVI.

ILLUSTRATIONS.

A 2

MY APINGI KINGDOM.

CHAPTER I.

TO MY YOUNG FRIENDS.

Dear Young Folks,—Here I am again with another book. I like to write for you, because you seem to enjoy my books, and so eagerly read all that I have to say to you.

In Lost in the Jungle I left you in Apingi Land, a country situated near the equator, and south of it. There the people were strange and superstitious. They were surrounded by immense forests, high mountains, and a large river flowed through their country. You will remember that at last they made me their king, and, as you know, it was in my kingdom that I left you, promising to come back to you in another year.

I keep my promise, and I am now going to tell you more about that Apingi Land, and what I did there, and afterwards I will take you to the great Desert, and we will have a cruise together along the western coast of Africa.

CHAPTER II.

A COUNCIL.—SHALL WE BUILD A HUNDRED CANOES.—THE GREAT FALLS OF SAMBA-NAGOSHI.—FOUGAMOU, THE FORGER OF IRON.—PEOPLE CAN NOT SEE HIM WORK IRON; IF THEY DO, THEY DIE.

After the scenes I have described to you in the preceding volumes, and by which you saw with what degree of superstition the people looked upon me, I need not tell you that I was the most powerful man in the country. The superstitious natives thought me to be a mighty spirit. Their king I was, and they respected me, and it was my aim to deserve their respect and love. I remembered the good precepts my mother had tried to teach me in my boyhood.

I cultivated with them truthfulness and kindness of heart. I took care of their sick, I loved their children, I prevented their women from being beaten; I made them feel they could rely upon my word, so that when I promised a thing would be done they knew it would be done. I was firm at the same time. I had to be politic, and there were customs and superstitions which I disliked, but which I knew time and education alone could destroy.

Remandji, his people, and the whole of the Apingi nation seemed to love me more and more as time passed on. I had some glorious talks with them, and every day I learned more of their people, superstitions, and customs. I loved to talk with those old men, and they loved to talk with me, and to ask me questions about the land of the Moguizi. Every day we had a talk together. Their men would bring them their palm wine, and they would gradually sip it, just as the Germans do their beer, and jabber away at the same time.

One sultry afternoon, when the rays of the sun were pouring down upon the forest, and making the heat intense in the village, Remandji, a few old men, and myself went towards the river, and, after reaching its banks, we seated ourselves under a very wide-spreading tree, with the big stream rolling at our feet. The water was yellow and turbid, for the rains had been heavy for a few days past.

After we had seated ourselves comfortably on some

WE ARE IN COUNCIL.

logs of wood that were lying on the ground—although I did not seat myself before I had examined my log well, for centipedes and scorpions are often found in the cracks of these dead pieces of wood—I began to question them.

"Remandji," said I, "suppose you build one hundred large canoes, while I go to the sea-shore and bring back to you and the Apingi large quantities of guns and swords. Then, after my return, suppose we load our canoes with palm oil, India-rubber, ebony wood, ivory, gum copal, and then go down the river to the sea and trade these products, and bring back all kinds of things that the people like, and would exchange for them.

"What do you think of this?" I said to him, looking him steadily but gently in the face, for I wanted to know his own thoughts, not by what he was going to say, but by the expression he would show.

Remandji and the old men round him began to look thoughtful, and seemed for a while to be lost in reflection.

Then Remandji said: "Spirit, the question you ask is a big thing. There are a great many tribes of wild and fighting men living on the banks of that big river that flows at our feet, and no one has ever tried to do what you propose. If you were to fly away, what would become of us? The whole country would be against us; tribe after tribe would fight us, for they would all say, 'How do the Apingi dare to come down the river and pass us?' I will tell you, Spirit, the names of some of the strange people who live on the banks of the river below us."

I must confess that some of these names were hard to pronounce, and if I had not written them down in my journal I should certainly have forgotten them. I give some of them to you, for I want you to know the names of some of the tribes inhabiting the banks of the big river by which we stood — the Kambas, Aviia, Osounga, Njavi; our old friends the Bakalai, of whom you have been made thoroughly well acquainted with in STORIES OF THE GORILLA COUNTRY, WILD LIFE UNDER THE EQUATOR, and LOST IN THE JUNGLE; Anenga, Ngaloi, Adjomba, and the Ogobai people. "These Ngalois, Anenga, Adjomba, and Ogobai people would fight us all the time," said Remandji, "for they have sworn, before our fathers were born, that no people from the up river should pass their tribe to go down; and who knows, perhaps, but that they would call all the people belonging to another river much bigger than ours, which is called Rembo Okanda, to come and join them and fight against us? Oh, Spirit, they are mighty fighting men on the Rembo Okanda River."

Then there was a pause. Remandji looked thoughtfully on the ground, and then, gradually raising his eyes, looked at me, and said again:

"I know that you want to make the Apingi people a great people; but what you said can not be done, for there is, lower down in the river, something more formidable, more terrible than all the wild people I have spoken of."

He looked at me to see if I knew what it was, when suddenly I shouted, "Do you mean the Samba-Nagoshi Falls?" for I had heard of them from the people of the sea-shore. Their fame was greater even than that of the Nkoumou-Naboulai Mountains, the summit of which I had tried to reach, of which enterprise you have had an account already.

"Yes," said Remandji; "no man can pass through the Samba-Nagoshi. No Apingi would dare to come near it, for there is death there, and mighty spirits reside there, who guard the river."

"Tell me," said I to Remandji, "tell me about the Samba-Nagoshi Falls. I want to hear what you have to say about them."

Remandji then fixed himself comfortably for a long speech, and began as follows:

"In the days of old, long, long ago, there was a great spirit living in the forest, whose name was Fougamou. Fougamou was a great forger of iron, and a mighty spirit. One day, as Fougamou was wandering through the great forest, he came upon the banks of our river, and made up his mind to dwell by it. At last the people began to find out that Fougamou would work iron for them. So, when any one wanted a spear or a hatchet, battle-axe, knife, or any other implement, he would go near the banks of the river, and cry, 'Oh! mighty Fougamou, I want this iron to be forged;' and then he named the instrument he wanted, as he deposited the rough iron he had dug up on the ground. Then he departed, for no one could ever see Fougamou work the iron, for Fougamou had forbidden people ever to look at him, and the people were afraid to do it, as they believed that if ever they saw him they would die.

"The following morning, when they went back to the place where they had deposited the iron, they would find the weapon they had asked for finished. So I need not tell you, Spirit, how much Fougamou was loved by the people.

"When Fougamou came to live on the banks of the

river, he said to himself that no one should ever go down or up the river in canoes, and he made a mighty barrier across the river, made of stone; and the water tumbles down and runs so fast," said Remandji, with a shudder, "that if a canoe was to be carried over the falls it would be broken in pieces, and the people killed. I wish you could hear the roaring water of Fougamou.

"Listen," added Remandji, observing that I was about to speak; "I have not finished the story of this great spirit.

"One day, however, a man and his son went in the forest with their iron and charcoal to ask Fougamou to work it for them, but they had made up their mind, before starting, that they would see Fougamou work the iron, and find out how it was done, and they said, 'Surely we shall not die if we see him.'

"So, after going for a long while through the forest, they came to the spot where the people were in the habit of depositing the iron. After leaving it and the charcoal on the ground, they hid themselves, the father in the hollow of a tree, and the son among the boughs of another tree. Fougamou came with his son, for Fougamou had a child, and began to work, when suddenly the son said, 'Father, I smell the smell of people.' The father replied, 'Of course you smell people; for does not the iron and charcoal come from the hands of people?' So they worked on. But the son again interrupted his father, saying again, 'Father, I do smell the smell of people.' Then Fougamou began to look round, thinking that what his son told him might be true. Then he saw the two men. He roared with rage till his roar shook the whole forest; and then, to punish the father and his son, he turned the tree in which the father was hidden into an ant-hill, and the hiding-place of the son into a nest of black ants. But," added Remandji, with a great sigh, "since then Fougamou has never worked iron. These two people were aniemba ("wizards"), for they broke the law Fougamou had made, and did not wish Fougamou to work iron any more for the people. But, like in the days of old, he still keeps the river.

"But, besides the great Fougamou, there are two other spirits who live by the river, and they also have made the river such that no canoe can pass. These two spirits are Samba and Nagoshi. Nagoshi is the wife of Samba."

After hearing the interesting legend of Samba-Nagoshi, I was surprised that time had gone on so rapidly. The sun had disappeared behind the trees, and darkness was soon to succeed daylight. The birds were looking for the trees they intended to rest upon for the night. Flocks of parrots were making for different parts of the forest. The insects were seeking for the leaves where they were going to take shelter, and the butterflies had become quiet.

How quickly time had fled! What strange "talks" I had heard!

So we got up and made for the village. When we entered it the people seemed glad to see us again, and I heard them say, "Look how the Spirit seems to love Remandji!"

CHAPTER III.

PREPARATIONS FOR HUNTING.—PEOPLE ORDERED TO GET READY.—THE IDOL IS PUT IN THE STREET.—DANCE WITH TORCHLIGHTS.—THE IDOL SAYS WE WILL KILL GAME.—THE PEOPLE BELIEVE IT.

If you had been in the Apingi country on that same evening of the day when I heard the legend of the Fougamou and Samba-Nagoshi, which I have just related to you, you would have seen me under the little veranda of Remandji's hut, seated quietly by his side, and talking to him. Remandji is a great smoker, and did really enjoy his pipe. It was a splendid pipe, made of clay, and he smoked through a long reed, the pipe resting on the ground. It really did me good also to see Remandji enjoy his pipe. I was almost sorry I could not keep him company, but I do not use tobacco in any form.

We were talking about a hunt to be made. He said, "Moguizi, at some distance from our village we have built a fence in the forest with little sticks about so high;" then he raised his hand to show me how high it was, and I judged it was about five or six feet, and he added that it was of great length, but could not tell how long. He said it was many and many a time longer than the village. We built this fence the last rainy season, and from place to place, not far from each other, there are kind of *loop-holes*, in which the game we chase before us goes in, and then can not get out.

"The day after to-morrow," said he, "if you like we will form a large party to drive the game into there. To-morrow we will collect food, and start early the next morning. We will take a hunting path which passes through the fence, and we will continue to travel to the other side till we are a good long way from it, then we will sleep in the woods, and the next morning will separate from each other, but you and I will remain together."

The old men around us agreed to this, and people were sent to many of the Apingi villages to tell the inhabitants that the second day afterward they must come to our village, for the Spirit wanted to go and hunt, and Remandji was going with him.

That same evening I furbished up a double-barreled smooth-bore gun, which I intended to load with buckshot for gazelles. Then I prepared another gun, which was to be loaded with bullets for larger game, such as elephants, gorillas, leopards, etc. In the afternoon hundreds of people came into the village; they were the men that were to start with Remandji and me for the hunt.

I remember well that night before our departure, though several years have passed since then. The night was clear, the stars were bright, and only a few fleecy white clouds, which moved overhead slowly, were to be seen. The huge idol, at eight o'clock by my watch, was taken from its house and put in front of it. Soon the moon rose, and its bright light shone upon the street, and every Apingi hut could be seen distinctly. Back of the huts the trees cast their huge shadows, and I could hear the whisper of the wind as it blew through the forest and over the village. The huge bats, commonly called vampires, flew above our heads as they passed into the forest to hang themselves to the branches of the trees. What a queer cry they had! How strangely sounded the noise they made! The croaking of frogs in the neighboring swamps could be distinctly heard. That part of the village where I stood was almost as quiet as the night itself, for all the villagers and the strangers had gone to the other end, and were no doubt talking over their stories, or discussing the plans of the hunt for the morrow.

I was facing the idol, and thought what an ugly thing it was. It was a female, about three feet in height, carved of wood, having a tremendous chest, which was full of charmed powder. Its head-dress was made of the little bristles from the tail of a porcupine. It wore a necklace made of the teeth of monkeys; the eyes were made of pieces of polished iron; round its waist it had a belt of feathers of wild guinea-fowl, while at its feet lay skulls of monkeys and of other wild animals.

As I was looking at this strange, ugly thing, I wondered how it was that men could believe that such things, made with their own hands, could talk, walk, eat, and wink their eyes, and work their vengeance on people; but then I remembered that there were once nations far higher in civilization than these poor creatures, people who have left to us noble and magnificent works of art and skill, who were equally imbued with the same folly and superstition. As I stood there thinking of these strange things, friend Remandji came to me and said that the crowd were coming to dance round the idol, and ask it to make us have plenty of game.

After a while great numbers of people came with

drums, and with a great quantity of torches made of the pitch produced from a certain tree. These were lighted and stuck in the ground surrounding the idol, excepting that there was a spot left open in front for the people to come close, so that they might speak to it. How strange the lurid glare of these torches made the idol appear! By the peculiar light the wooden god looked ten times as ugly as it appeared before.

About twenty yards in front of it the drummers put themselves in a row. There were about fifty of them, and they began to beat their drums, and the people began to sing to the idol, and promised to bring to it a great quantity of game, if they were fortunate enough to kill much.

Towards one o'clock in the morning the number of drummers and dancers became less and less, till at last no one was left on the dancing-ground but the idol. The next morning many of the villagers swore that during the night the idol walked in the street, and spoke aloud, and told the people that a large quantity of game was to be caught in the chase. So every body was joyous, and soon every thing was ready for our departure.

DANCING BEFORE THE IDOL.

CHAPTER IV.

PORCUPINE HUNTING.—THEY COME OUT OF THEIR BURROWS. —FIERCE ATTACK OF THE DOGS.—PORCUPINE TRAPS.—THE LEGEND OF THE PORCUPINE AND OF THE LEOPARD.

Early on the morning of the scene just described to you in the preceding chapter, Okabi and I resolved to go to a place not far from the village, which he had discovered while rambling in the forest, where porcupines were abundant. So we left, taking with us four dogs, and after about an hour's walk we came to a place in the forest, near the bottom of a hill, where the ground was very stony. It was not long before I discovered many burrows where the creatures were hidden. The dogs at once began to bark furiously at the entrance of the burrows, and to try to get in by scratching away the earth. The porcupine being a nocturnal animal, they had all retired into their holes. But we should have had to wait long if we had waited for the dogs to dig them out. We had provided ourselves with an implement for digging, and went to work in good earnest at one of the burrows. We soon started one of the animals, and off he went on a run, with the dogs after him. They speedily overtook him, and barked and jumped briskly round him, but were afraid to touch the creature. I did not blame them, for it would have done no good. This was a big one, and his long, sharp-pointed quills spread rapidly, and protected the animal as if they were so many bayonets. His little tufted tail, which was covered with most extraordinary little balls of quills of a yellowish color, which at first sight look like a horny substance or thick parchment, rattled as the porcupine moved about; and, if I had been in the land of rattlesnakes, and had not seen the porcupine, I might have then thought that one was near at hand. Some of the quills in the middle of the creature's back are five and six inches long, and sometimes even longer. They are very sharply pointed. There was no fear of the dogs getting hold of him. Indeed, no animal would relish such a mouthful. Neither the leopards nor hyenas would venture upon it. The dogs knew that it was of no use for them to try, and hence they were mad. We could not help laughing to see them. Their hair stood right up, so furious were they, so that their backs almost appeared like that of the porcupine, only with short quills. They would come near and bark furiously, show their teeth, and then back out. Finally the porcupine turned round, and, having a stone to protect him, showed fight; this made the dogs bark more furiously than ever. Nothing but a smart blow on the head of the porcupine would kill him, for we could not take hold of the animal with our hands. His quills would have gone through them. Seizing a piece of wood, I just gave the fellow a stunning blow on his head, which laid him out on the ground, and another blow on the head again finished him.

I saw that the longest quills were flexible, and could not do much harm to an enemy, the shorter ones being stiff. The porcupine feeds on roots, leaves, nuts, and different vegetable productions. The quills of the por-

PORCUPINE HUNT.

cupine are often used as pen-holders, and very pretty ones they make.

They come out of their burrows about sunset, and wander during the night. When the natives have discovered a porcupine burrow, which is sometimes very deep, they set a trap that is so constructed that it catches the animal when it comes out. This trap is made of the bough of a tree, one end of which is firmly fixed on the ground; the other extremity is bent forward, and to it is attached a noose with a slip-knot just over the opening of the burrow. The porcupine, in coming out, puts his head into this noose, and at the same time loosens a peg that holds the spring lightly by pushing forward, and up he goes into the air, hung by the neck. The noose grows tighter and tighter the more he moves and shakes, and soon strangles him to death. I have often seen porcupines trapped in this way.

Immediately after the first blow the quills began to drop down flat on its back; at the second blow the animal was killed.

After killing two more porcupines we returned to the village. A little after my arrival I found that there was to be a fight among the villagers. They all wanted the tails of the porcupines, and every body thought he had a right to them. Every body was shouting at the top of his voice, as if they thought the one who could make the most noise had the best right to the spoils. This great fuss was made on account of the porcupines' tails being used for fetiches or charms. I stopped the noise by saying that if there were a fight for these tails, I should join in it, and knock down right and left. This talk of mine put a stop to their quarrel; and, in order to satisfy them and make them good-natured, I appropriated the three tails myself, so there might be no jealousy.

The porcupine is really good to eat. Having some nice, fresh palm oil, made the day before from nuts we had collected, I cooked my share in the oil, and, having seasoned it with salt and plenty of Cayenne pepper, I had a splendid dinner.

As we had been hunting porcupines all the morning, we were bound to have a porcupine story on my return. Okabi was a real good story-teller, and so he began:

"A long time ago, when my father was a boy, one day he got very greatly scared. He was coming back to the village from the forest, where he had gone in search of wild honey, when he suddenly saw, near the hunting path, an immense leopard lying flat on the ground. The leopard's back was turned towards him, and so the creature did not see him. His long tail wagged to and fro, and he lay very quiet. Father, seeing a big hollow tree close to him, hid himself in it. But he did not feel safe. He was afraid to stir or make any sound, for fear of alarming the leopard and betraying himself. Looking closely, he saw that the leopard was watching a porcupine about a yard in front of his nose. The poor porcupine was all drawn up in a bunch. His quills were all standing out like so many sharp-pointed spears, and it was evident that both were at a stand-still. The leopard, not a bit frightened, seemed to be lying in wait for the proper time to kill his prey, while the porcupine, knowing full well that, if it did not keep on the defensive, or tried to escape, the leopard would turn him over with one stroke of his huge paw, and expose the under part of his body, which is soft and undefended with quills. He would then fall an easy prey to the leopard's sharp claws. So the porcupine stood still, rolled up so tight that he could hardly turn his head, and thoroughly protected by his bristling quills.

"My father saw the leopard now and then try, with its big long paw, to draw the porcupine towards him, but he would instantly take it off, the quills pricking him in a way he did not like at all. There the leopard lay and lay, till at last he got up, and father became very much afraid, for he knew not if the leopard had smelt him. Nothing," said Okabi, "saved him but the monda (fetich) which he wore, and which came from my grandfather, for grandfather was a great hunter and a daring warrior." The people shouted with one voice, "So he was."

"The leopard, after a great while, went away, but not

without giving a fearful growl of disappointment, but it was long before father left his hiding-place, being afraid of the treachery of the leopard, for they are not to be trusted. It was a long time before the porcupine moved away, and my father did not want to kill him, 'for,' said he, 'the porcupine has escaped from such a dangerous enemy, why should I kill him?'"

I was quite ready for the great hunt to come off in the morning, and went to sleep, having before my eyes visions of great quantities of game.

CHAPTER V.

THE SPIRIT, OUR KING. — GREAT NUMBER OF PLAINTAIN-TREES.—CURIOUS FENCE FOR GAME.—WE MARCH SILENTLY. — WE SURROUND OURSELVES WITH FIRES. — THE STRANGE LEGEND OF ARONDO-IÉNOU.

THE next morning the cries of the wild guinea-fowls which had come near the village awoke me. It was just daylight. The birds had come down from the trees where they had perched for the night, and were wandering in the neighboring jungle. I immediately jumped from my bed. It took but little time to dress, for my coat and my shoes were the only part of my clothing I had removed on lying down. By my side lay two of my guns. Taking a gun with me, I went to a little stream meandering not far from the village, and washed my face in its cool and clear water.

On my return I found that all the villagers were awake, and busy getting ready for our hunting trip. Remandji was standing before my hut, and, as soon as I made my appearance, they all shouted, "The Spirit, our king, is coming."

Every one loaded himself with his own provisions with the exception of Remandji and myself, and some of the boys carried the provisions of their fathers or uncles in queer-looking bags. So we started. Several wives of the king accompanied us. Our way was along a narrow hunting path which led us through some splendid plantations of plantain-trees and of cassada, which were worked by Remandji's wives and slaves. Now and then we crossed through large patches of sugar-cane, planted also by Remandji's wives. Two or three days before, the chimpanzees had come in large numbers and eaten a great quantity of it. Many patches of canes had been torn up and partly destroyed on the spot. The Apingi and Remandji cursed the chimpanzees as we passed by the half-destroyed patches of the cane.

After going through thousands and thousands of plantain-trees, we took a hunting path, and, after a walk of about three hours, we came to the "fence," which I examined carefully. The fence appeared to me like a miniature wall surrounding a fortified town; it was about six feet in height, and every twenty or thirty yards there was a cul de sac. Each of these was about ten or twelve feet in length, about eighteen inches or two feet broad at the opening, and gradually narrowed toward the end, so that the game, once in, could not turn round to get out. The sticks were small, about six feet in height, stuck in the ground, and closely tied together by the help of creepers and lianes. This game fence was said to be of very great length.

We continued our march for at least three hours after we had passed the fence, keeping perfectly silent in the mean time, not a single man uttering a word, as we did not want to frighten the game away. At length we came to a spot where there was a large clearing, which had been made by the natives. I could see at once that the spot was a rendezvous for hunting parties, as there were remains of old fires all about, and I saw the bones of wild animals which had been eaten before scattered on the ground. Sheds had also been constructed of large boughs, thatched with leaves, to protect the people from the heavy rains.

On each side of the camp ran a hunting path, which diverged from the one we had come by. One of these hunting paths ran straightly to the left, and the other to the right—that is, one went directly north, while the other went directly south. The path we had taken from Remandji ran almost eastward. The game fence we had passed ran, as I had been given to understand, south and north, so I came to the conclusion that these two paths were running parallel with the fence. When I asked Remandji, I saw that I was not mistaken.

This encampment which we had just reached was the spot where we were to spend the night; so some of the men went immediately to work and collected a large quantity of firewood, while others went after large leaves to repair the sheds, which were somewhat dilapidated, as it had been a long time since the Apingi had come here. Remandji and I had our sheds close to each other. I lighted four fires, one at my head, one on my left, another on my right, and another at my feet. I always liked to surround myself with fire, for I did not fancy the snakes which often crawl about at night, and, above all, I did not fancy to be carried away in the jaws of a leopard, for there is no way to get out of a leopard's jaw after you are there, and I did not care in the least to be carried off in that manner, and be devoured by such a monster. I thought this would be no joke, and I am sure, my dear young folks, you think just as I do. Leopards were plentiful, and the Apingi took great care to light a great many fires, for all wild beasts are afraid of fire.

Each man cooked his own meal—that is to say, every one roasted his plantain and his meat, which was either a dry piece of elephant, some smoked monkey, snake, or fish—about bright charcoal fires. So the fragrance of our cooking spread from one end of the camp to the other.

After our meal the time to tell stories came, and I am going to tell you one or two which were interesting to me, and may prove so to you. Okabi was to be the spokesman.

"Atoongouloo-Shimba was a king, having come to his kingdom by law of inheritance. Atoongouloo had made up his mind that whoever should quarrel in his dominions he would eat. After eating people after people, he was left all alone. A neighboring king, called Koniambié, had a beautiful child, named Arondo-Iénou. Atoongouloo-Shimba married this daughter of Koniambié, and, after he had put the rings on her legs,* he started for the forest, to catch wild beasts with the Ashinga net, leaving his wife alone in the village.

"Koniambié, besides Arondo-Iénou, had three children—three boys. The eldest was called Ndjali (gun or thunder). Ndjali said he was going to take back from Atoongouloo-Shimba his sister, and Atoongouloo-Shimba ate Ndjali, who had come to take away his wife from him. He ate also the second brother. When a woman has several children, the last one is called Reninga. So Re-

* The putting of rings on the legs is like the giving of the wedding ring among us.

ninga came to take away his sister, and he and Atoongouloo-Shimba fought and fought from morning till the sun reached the meridian, but finally Atoongouloo succeeded in eating Reninga; but Reninga had a fetich, and came out of Atoongouloo-Shimba alive.*

"When the latter saw this, he said, 'What are you coming back for?' Then he put the chalk of the Alumbi on Reninga and Arondo-Iénou; then, joining their hands together, he blew a breath upon them, and said to Reninga, 'Take your sister away.' Then Reninga took his sister away. After that, Atoongouloo-Shimba drowned himself, because his wife had been taken away from him. But, before dying, he said to Reninga, 'If Arondo-Iénou ever marries another man, she will die.' Arondo-Iénou did not believe the saying of Reninga, and married another man, and she at once died.

"At the place where Atoongouloo drowned himself, when a stranger looks in the water he sees in the deep the body of Arondo-Iénou, and her nails appear like looking-glass.

"Since that time water is often called Arondo-Iénou, because people can see their own likeness in it on account of the nails of Arondo-Iénou. Before the death of Arondo-Iénou, the water could not reflect the image of people."

* They have all sorts of monda, "fetiches, gree-grees," many of which are supposed to work miracles.

CHAPTER VI.

DIFFICULT HUNTING PATH.—THE MEN SCATTER.—REMANDJI AND MYSELF REMAIN TOGETHER.—FEAR OF ELEPHANTS.—CAPTURE OF GAME.—SNAKES ARE KILLED.

At daylight we were all up and ready. We divided ourselves into two parties; one took the path which led northward, and the other the path which led southward. Remandji and I belonged to the southern party. We were equally divided in number, each side having about three hundred people.

I saw by my compass that we were going directly south. Remandji and I, with a few other men, who were his nephews, kept in the rear of our line. This hunting path was an awful one. It had not been used for a long time, and the jungle had overgrown and covered it, and there were great numbers of fallen trees in our way, and some of these were so very big that I can assure you it was no joke to climb over them or go under them. It became very wearisome. After a while, every twenty or thirty yards more or less, we would station a man in the path, to remain there till he heard the horn sound, which was the signal to advance forward toward the west, that is to say, toward the fence. At length half of the men of our party had been left at different points along the road. Remandji and I and two of his nephews halted, and let the remainder pass us and go ahead, as we wished to remain about in the centre. Those who passed us were to leave men, as had been done before, till none were left. Okabi was their leader. We were to keep perfectly still; not a man was to utter a word. Then, when the last man was posted, Okabi was to sound the horn, and those who had horns along the line were to answer the signal.

The other half of our party, which had taken the northern path, had been doing exactly what we had done. At certain distances apart they had stationed their horn-men, who were to answer as soon as they heard the horns from our side, as that would be the signal that there were no more men to station, and that every one was ready to advance toward the fence. Remandji and I, who were at the centre of the line, waited at least one hour before the horn sounded; of course we did not hear the most distant horns, but, as soon as the farther one was blown, the one nearest to it answered, and so on, till at last the signal was sounded all along the line, from the last man south to the last man north. This was the signal that every thing was ready. Then we advanced, each man straight before him westward, that is to say, right toward the fence. We shouted, we hallooed, each man trying to shout louder than the rest. Our only fear was that elephants might lie between us and the fence, and that in running away they would break through the obstructions, and that the smaller game would go through the gaps the elephants would make, and then escape from us.

We were, I thought, about six or seven miles from the fence. Steadily we advanced through the thick jungle, which at times was terribly close; and the only way we knew that we were going straight was by the many small branches of young trees which had been broken by parties who had been hunting here before us.

Of course the game fled before us, for the great noise we made frightened them very much; but, as they could run faster through the forest than we could, we did not expect to come to a fight or a slaughter before we reached the fence. Our only fear, as I said, was that elephants were between us and the fence. If it was so, we should not get much game, and perhaps might lose it all.

Steadily, slowly, but surely we came nearer and nearer the fence. At last a wild shout ran along the line. The fence came in sight, and what a sight it was! Wild beasts of all kinds were running to and fro, mad with terror. Hyenas, porcupines, black wild boars, gazelles, antelopes, wild cats, and even snakes were driven helter-skelter within the inclosure. They would run along the fence till they came to the long *pouches*, or cul de sac, and, thinking these were ways of escape, into them they would go, and find they were snared.

The spears of the Apingi went through the animals along the whole line. The slaughter was terrific. My first shot was for a very large snake, some nineteen feet long, a python, which, seeing that he could not get through the fence, made in my direction, and was spreading terror and dismay among the Apingi, for it had its mouth wide open, its sharp-pointed tongue was thrust a long way out, and its hissing could even be heard in the midst of the uproar that raged around us.

I was glad that we had not been troubled by elephants.

APINGI GAME FENCE.

I immediately advanced, after reloading the barrel I had fired. There was a savage black boar, whose sharp muzzle had been thrust between the sticks of the fence, so that he was in a fair way to get through, but a shot of mine put an end to its life. A fine fat creature it was. I suddenly saw an ugly big wild cat, at which an Apingi had hurled a spear, but had missed him. The creature, being brought to bay, was about to spring upon his assailant, when, in a jiffy, I brought him down, in the midst of the great cheers of those around us.

The *cul de sac*, which, according to the hunting laws, belonged to me, was filled with gazelles, which were immediately speared by the Apingi. There was a porcupine among them, which could not have been at all a pleasant companion to the gazelles. It would be hard to say which of the creatures was the most frightened.

The excitement all along the line was intense, and the loud shouts of the Apingi sounded strangely in the woods. But at last all quieted down again. All the game worth killing had been killed, and whatever was too large for a single man to carry was cut up in small pieces. Then, taking up our line of march, we followed the fence, and advanced toward the same main path from which we had separated, and before evening we were in our camping-ground of the day before. There we all met and counted the spoils. The slaughter of wild beasts had been very great. There were six wild black boars, twenty-three gazelles, seven porcupines, five wild cats, three hyenas, seven red antelopes, and three huge snakes. These last were to be cooked in plantain leaves, with lemon-juice and plenty of Cayenne pepper, of which there is a great abundance in the country.

After every body had arrived a tremendous wild shout of joy rang through the woods. What a pile of game there was! The mouths of the Apingi extended from ear to ear, and showed their sharp-pointed, filed teeth. They were right glad of the prospect of a good supper.

It was agreed that the game should be divided that evening among us. Remandji and I were to superintend the distribution. Of course, in that part of the world, it would not have done to give to each an equal share, for it would have been against the customs of the people. So we gave only to the heads of the families, and these were to divide the meat, according to their own will and pleasure, among the younger retainers, nephews, sons, and cousins, as they should think best. The head of a family is thought a great deal of in that wild part of the world.

With Remandji's people and mine there was no quarreling; but, my goodness! I wish you could have heard the Apingi quarreling among themselves. Not one of them was satisfied with his share. Every one thought that his neighbor had a better share than himself. Of course the heads of families took the lion's share. Remandji and myself each took a whole boar. These black boars are not so large as the yellow ones I have described to you in former volumes, and are far from being so nice-looking.

We slept that night where we had divided the game. The forest was full of the smell of roasted meat, for there was not a man there who thought that his wife would be glad to have a piece of his meat. Women, they think, must eat when their husbands are not hungry, and the children when the mothers are satisfied.

The wives never eat with their husbands, and it is but seldom, if ever, that grown-up sons and nephews eat with their fathers and uncles. They are supposed to be too young, and it would not be considered respectful for them to eat with their elders. So that what is left of a meal the wives eat, and what the wives leave the children eat; if there is nothing for them, they must do the best they can to find food, or go hungry, as they like best.

CHAPTER VII.

DEPARTURE TO VISIT MY DOMINIONS.—PRECEDED BY ONE HUNDRED HORN-MEN.—FOLLOWED BY MY HOUSEKEEPER. —WAR MUST NOT TAKE PLACE.—I GET IN A FURIOUS RAGE.—HAPPY DENOUEMENT.

THE day after my return from our hunting expedition, I thought it was time for me to visit the villages belonging to the country over which I had been made king; so I spoke to Remandji, who was, if I may use the expression, my minister, or major general, and the people were ordered to get ready to start the next day.

I wanted to learn the resources of the country; see what the people could do, what they manufactured, and what the agricultural productions were, and thus become acquainted with the sort of commerce to which the country was best adapted. I must explore the forests to find out what precious woods they contained, and if we could obtain valuable gums and minerals for our market. It was arranged that I should leave with a large retinue of followers. My procession was to be headed by a band of more than one hundred horn-men. The natives are very fond of blowing these horns, and many of them have been handed down from father to son for several generations. They are from one to two feet in length, and are made of the horns of an antelope called the kambi. The kambi is a species of antelope, of a gray color, with whitish stripes on the sides. The full-grown specimens are almost as large as a cow. The business of the horn-men was to sound the horn whenever we ap-

THE BLOWING OF KAMBI HORNS.

proached a village, in order to let the people know I was coming. All the horn-men were painted with yellow, red, and white ochre, and covered with their fetiches. Remandji himself was to be followed by almost all his sons and many of his wives. They also were all covered with fetiches, and all invoked the Spirit of the Alumbi to be with them.

Remandji insisted that I should take my splendid

housekeeper with me, whose likeness you saw in my last volume. "For," said he, "she must take care of you; she has nothing else to do but to get your food ready, to watch over you, to drive the flies away during your sleep, to fetch water for you, and to scratch your head when you want it done." I did not like the insinuation in the last part of Remandji's speech, and I said to him, "You know very well that I have nothing on my head."

"But you know," replied Remandji, "that it would be a disgrace to me if she did not follow you." So I gave way at last to the earnest entreaties of Remandji, and it was agreed that my housekeeper should follow me. It was of no use for me to fight against it. I could not get rid of her.

The following morning there was a great stir in the village, for we were all prepared to start. As I was getting ready, what should I see but my beautiful housekeeper. She, too, was ready, and was bound not to let us go without her. The order for departure at length arrived. I wore on my shoulder my emblem of royalty (the "kendo"), of which I gave you a description and picture in my last volume. I was followed by Remandji. I took the kendo from my shoulder, and rang it. There was a dead silence at once, and then a wild shout, "The Spirit, our king, is going to speak!" rung through the village. In order to impress them with awe, I fired two guns, loaded with tremendous charges of powder, which made a very loud report. Then, taking hold of my revolvers, I fired and fired in the air. The Apingi fell upon the ground, filled with fear. Remandji bowed down in front of me, and looked me steadily in the face. The people all at once began to sing, "Oh Spirit, oh

Spirit, thou art our king. Oh Spirit, oh Spirit, we never saw thee before. Oh Spirit, oh Spirit, do not send disease and death among us. Oh Spirit, all the beasts of the forest will come to thee! Oh Spirit, now thou art going to visit all the Apingi land. Oh Spirit, we say good-by to thee! Oh Spirit, oh Spirit, we will wait for thee. Remandji goes with thee—take care of him. Many of our people go with thee—oh take care of them all." Then the horns blew again, and what a noise they made! And with the drums beating in the village, we soon disappeared in the forest, amid the wild shouts of the people that had remained behind. Forty Apingi warriors, armed with spears, took the lead, then the horn-men, and immediately after came Remandji and myself, followed by the women, and also some warriors as a rear-guard.

It was easy to see that we were not going on a hunting expedition.

After walking about an hour and a half, the horn-men again began to blow their horns, and a wild Apingi shout followed up. We were approaching a village. Soon we came in sight of it, and then all the horn-men sounded the horns, and all the party shouted, "The great Spirit is coming to you. Remandji is with him. Be not afraid." When we came to the village there was not a soul in sight. The people had all gone inside of their houses. They were afraid till the voice of Remandji bade them take courage, and then, one by one, they came out. In the mean time I went to the ouandja, and there waited. I fired two guns to announce my arrival. In the mean time the people had all assembled at the extreme end of the village, but as soon as they heard the guns they bent themselves low, and, in a hopping sort of a way, they advanced toward me, singing songs of praise. They carried their huge idol with them; and finally, when they came quite close, they put the Mbuiti ("idol") before me, and said to it, "Look at the Spirit! Behold, look at the Spirit! Look, look at our king!" This idol was the imitation of a man, and had been carved from a very large piece of wood. My goodness gracious! it did look ugly enough.

Then presents of food were brought before me, plantains, bananas, pine-apples, pea-nuts, fowls, dried fish, and a goat.

Remandji seemed to be in his glory. At night a grand ball was given in my honor, but, being somewhat weary, I retired early, for in the morning a great palaver was to take place, and I was to settle it.

Early the next morning I seated myself under a very large tree to receive the people of the village and hear the palaver. After a while the village drums began to beat. The drummers were at the other end of the village. Afterward the people began to sing, and at last I saw a crowd coming toward me. In the mean time Remandji had made his appearance, accompanied by the hundred horn-men, who began to blow their horns, so that, between the noise of the tam-tam and the music of the horns, I found myself in not a very quiet place. The chief of the village then came before me, followed by forty-three girls. He talked to Remandji, and said that he was so glad the Spirit had come to see him. Like the other chiefs with Remandji, he had made him their king. He himself was poor. He had not many things to give away, as the Spirit had, like the sand. The black man is poor. He has only plenty to eat, and his coat—pointing to mine—is his own skin. Then, turning himself toward me, he said, "Here are forty-three nice girls. Some of them are my daughters, others are nieces, others are my childrens' children, and some are the children of the big men of my village. Take them, Spirit; we give them all to thee to be thy wives." There was a tremendous shout of approbation. Immediately the drums began to beat, the men began to blow their horns, and the people began to dance round me, and they danced and danced till I thought they must be crazy. Old Remandji himself got so excited that he could not withstand the temptation, and, getting on his feet, he cut up any amount of capers. The whole village was wild with excitement. Single persons would come and speak to me before the people with a sonorous voice, but I could not understand what they said. At last I fired a gun into the air. In an instant all became quiet, and I said, "Apingi, I will sleep in many of your villages; I will eat plantains with you, for I want you to remember me, for you made me your king. Now go away to your houses. When the sun will go down, when the heat of the day will have passed away, you will come back under this big tree, and if you have any palaver, Remandji and I will talk about it." The people at once scattered. I wondered what there was in me to fill these poor people with so much wonder and astonishment, and I thanked a kind Providence that took such great care of me, and that had directed my steps in such a manner that I could safely visit countries that had never been seen before by civilized man.

To my utter astonishment, when the people went away, the forty-three girls did not move. I remembered that I had not said a word about them. It was evident they considered themselves my wives, as they had been given away to me. Woman in that country has no will of her own; her father, uncles, and other male members of her family have to guide her and tell her what to do; so, if I was willing, they were to belong to me. While I was thinking it over they all got into a quarrel, as the old housekeeper insisted on being the head of them all, and I wandered away, leaving them to settle the dispute among themselves.

When I returned to my seat under the big tree in the afternoon, the women were still there waiting for me, just as I had left them in the morning. The quarrel was not settled, and the old housekeeper was still cross and ugly. Then the villagers came about me again. I said to them, "I must go. I have slept in your village one night, and now I must go to see other villages." But the people, as soon as they heard me, shouted, "Spirit, do not go away! Spirit, do not go away!" I rang my kendo as loud as I could to make them quiet, and, when silence was restored, told them that if there was trouble among them, if there was quarreling and palavers to settle, they must come to me and to Remandji, with the old men of villages, and we would settle them. They answered, "Good Spirit, we have no quarrel just now."

Then I got up, and, turning to the horn-blowers, I ordered them to blow the signal for our departure. The horns sounded, and I was ready to start for a village not far away. A short walk would take us there. But here a sad dilemma arose. "Oh Spirit," said the chief to me, "take all of thy wives with thee; they will follow thee through the Apingi country." And all the women began to sing, "We will follow the good Spirit through the Apingi country; we will prepare food for him; we will catch fish for him; we will fetch water for him; we will get wild berries for him!" And so they went on singing, and I thought I was merely going to have forty-three cooks to accompany me, for it seemed as if I could never get rid of them. But at last I pacified them by distributing a great number of trifling presents among them, and then took my departure amidst great cheering. I had not proceeded far on my route to the next village, however, when, turning round, I saw, to my great consternation, that we were followed by the forty-three women, and many warriors besides!

After walking about an hour I came to a queer village. There were very many huts, and the walls of these were built of the bark of trees, and the roofs were thatched with palm leaves. There were no windows, and only one door to each hut; they were all built alike, about ten feet long, and only seven or eight feet broad. The natives had been expecting us, and welcomed me with the sounds of drums, and with wild Apingi shouts. It was a big village, built in a single street. The name of the old man who was chief over the village was Andeko. I went to bed very early, for I was tired, and the noise they had made was so great. There was a dead silence during the night, for it was announced that the Spirit was tired, and wanted to rest.

Early the next morning I was awakened by wild shouts of war. I jumped from my couch, and, with my gun in hand, came out, looking as fierce as I could. I exclaimed, "Apingi, what do you mean? There must be no war among yourselves. Woe to the man who brings on war in the Apingi country, for I will slay him. I will kill him as sure as I kill that bird." For, luckily, just as I was speaking, a bird flew near the hut where I stood, and gave me the chance to impress the natives with a sense of my skill and power. I shot it flying, and it fell stone-dead just at the feet of the chief Andeko. A wild shout of fear was heard through the crowd, and many fled from me. "How can it be," they said, "that birds flying high in the sky should fall dead at our chief's feet when the great Spirit lets the thunder that he holds in his hands (meaning my gun) make a noise?" And then they sung, "Big Spirit, do not be angry. We do not want to make war. Some people want to make war upon us." I looked fierce, and, taking one of my revolvers in one hand, I fired and fired until the crowd shouted, "Spirit, our king, be not angry; Spirit, our king, do not kill the Apingi people."

Turning to Remandji, I said, "There must be no war. I must know the cause of this trouble." Then I rang my kendo, and ordered the people to come before me and I would hear the palaver.

They came, and brought before me a beautiful black girl; that is, she was beautiful for that country. I do not think you would say she was very handsome, for her teeth were filed into sharp points, and she was tattooed all over, Apingi fashion. She was young, only about fourteen years of age. Then they brought to her side a young man about twenty-four years of age. He was a nephew of the king. The young girl had fled from her own village one dark evening, in the midst of a tremendous rain-storm, and had come to this village. The name of the girl was Mishono, and the nephew of the king was called Ngooloo-Gani.

I eyed Mishono and Ngooloo-Gani with a look which

told them plainly that there could be no war on this occasion. While they stood before me they trembled all over.

Then the king said, "Oh Spirit, in our land, when a girl runs away from a village and comes to another, that village can not give her back without feeling shame. In the Apingi country we never give back a woman that comes to us. In her village, they want her to marry somebody she does not like, and she loves my nephew, and she thought she would rather run away than to go and marry where she does not want. She has *bola bongo*, 'put her hand on my head,' and you know this is our way of claiming protection; and how can I, without shame, give her back?" And the people all shouted, "How can we, without shame, give her back?"

This custom of adoption is a singular one, and prevails in all this part of Africa. When a man or woman runs away to another village, the first thing they have to do is to put themselves under the protection of some man. So, when they reach the place where they want to stay, they go to the man and put their hands upon his head, and this ceremony is called *bola bongo*. Henceforth they belong to the man, and he is bound to protect them. You will agree with me that this is a singular custom.

I questioned the girl, and she said, while tears rolled down her cheeks, "Spirit, I am afraid of thee. Oh, why did not I die the day I was born! Now I do not want to marry the man my people want me to marry. Women, oh Spirit, are shame in this country, and can be given away like goats and wild game, for our laws are such that her people do not ask whom she wants to marry.

She is even given away again after her husband is dead. After her time of mourning is past she has no choice, but must marry his brother, whether she likes him or not. If she does not, she had better not tell it, for she is flogged, and her body is torn with the whip. No, Spirit, I do not want to marry the man my people wants me to. I had rather be killed or be eaten up by the wild beasts. I do not want to go back." When she stopped speaking the people shouted, "We do not want to send her back, for shame would be upon us if we did; all the other villages would laugh at us, and call us 'chickens.' We do not want to be called chickens."

"Oh Spirit," said Mishono to me, "oh Spirit, do not be angry!" and the people also cried, "Oh Spirit, do not be angry! do not be angry!"

This was certainly a very complicated palaver, and in this part of Africa such things always bring on war. I wanted to avert war, and at the same time I had to give a just verdict. So I called Ngooloo-Gani, and said to him, "What have you to say for yourself?" "Spirit," said he, "this girl wants to marry me. She has run away from her village, and has *bola bongo* on the head of our chief, and it would be a great shame for our people to give her back, for we never do such a thing in the Apingi country; but in the moon, where you come from, you may have other fashions. Oh Spirit, do not be angry! Do not kill me!" Then the poor fellow kneeled down and got hold of my feet, which is, as you know, the most imploring way of asking a great favor in the region of Equatorial Africa.

I got up, and immediately ordered some Apingi to go and tell the people of the village where the girl came from, to come instantly to see me. I wanted to see the chief and the leading men, and I said, in order that they might not be afraid, "Two of you must remain in their village." So they went, and, as the village was not very far off, they came back in less than two hours, but with no one with them. The answer was that they did not want to talk the palaver. On receiving this message I rose to my feet, and, in a very loud tone of voice, began to speak in all the languages I knew—Apingi, Ashira, Commi, French, English, etc. I was very fierce. Oh, how they stared at me! "They dare me," I exclaimed. "They won't come when I bid them come!" I fired off my gun, I brandished it in the air, I flourished my revolver, I then rang my kendo, and told Remandji to prepare for a fight. Then I ordered the people of the village to go and fetch their spears, their battle-axes, and their bows and arrows, and their war-drums. The horns sounded the war tunes; messengers were sent to Remandji's village for more men to come. The idol was brought out, the men painted themselves and covered themselves with fetiches. "Onward, Apingi! onward for that village!" I shouted. Over three hundred men took the war-path. I led the way, and, as they followed, they sang their war-songs, and brandished their spears and their knives. When we approached the villages the war-songs were sung louder and louder, and the warriors became more exasperated. I was glad to see this, because I wanted to make an example. As we came nearer I heard the war-drums in the village, and the people shouting. I fired a gun into the air as I entered the village. I had put in a tremendous charge, and it went off with a fearful detonation. The recoil was so great that it almost knocked me down. The detonation resounded from hill to hill, and carried terror to the hearts of the timid villagers, who, at sight of us, retreated to the farther end, from which position they fled as we approached. But I told Remandji to shout to them not to be afraid. I did not come to kill them; they had made me their king. I was their father. A father did not kill his children unless the children wanted to make war. So Remandji shouted, "The Spirit bids you come. He does not want to kill you unless you dare to make war upon us. He comes to talk the palaver over the girl that ran away."

They had all fled, but at last the chief came again; for I sent word that if he did not come I would burn his village. He was followed by his head wife. I went toward him. On looking at him, I recognized him as one who had brought me food, and had been my friend. Round his neck he wore the beads which I had given him, and as bracelets he wore two brass rings which I had also given him. I went up to him, I shook hands with him, and told him not to be afraid, but to call his people together, as I had come to hold a palaver. So he went away, and a little while afterward came back with his people. We went under the big ouandja, and, after every body had seated himself, Remandji got up; and, addressing himself to the people, said, "The Spirit wanted to come and see you in peace, and you have threatened to make war. But it is a good thing that you did not make war, for you would have been all killed by this time. By the breath of his nostrils he would have sent death unto you all. You know that many of your daughters, sisters, and nieces are married in our villages, and that war between ourselves must not take place, for there are not two villages in the whole tribe that are more friendly with each other than yours and ours. The Spirit and I have held the palaver this morning. You know that one of the girls of our village is soon to marry a man of yours." Here Remandji called the man. He proved to be an old man, and I wondered why he wanted to marry. He was very ugly-looking. Half of his file-teeth had dropped out, and what were left were very black and dirty. Remandji went on: "Well, we will ask no dowry for that girl—no more slaves, no more goats, and no more things. So the palaver will be settled, and Mishono will remain with Ngooloo-Gani." There was a tremendous shout of "Yo! yo! yo!" which meant "Yes, that is so."

So this offer was accepted at once, for the parents of the girl in Remandji's village wanted from the old fellow I have just described to you two slaves, three goats, ten fowls, five cooking-dishes, three water-jars, five spears, and three large knives, before they would give away their daughter. So the people thought they had made a splendid bargain.

Immediately the two contending parties separated to a distance of about forty yards, then advanced with their spears in hand toward each other, just as if they were going to fight, uttering, at the same time, fierce Apingi shouts till they met; then the spears came down, the war-drums beat, the horns blew, the palaver was over, and I had stopped the threatened war. Then I presented the king with a waistcoat, which he wore in the midst of the most vociferous cheers of his people. That night there was a tremendous jollification in the real old Apingi style. A war-dance, and then all was over. Toward two o'clock in the morning all had become silent. The people had all returned, and nothing was to be heard except now and then the barking of the dogs, and the wild cries of hyenas lurking round in the forest. As I came out, as usual, to make an inspection of every thing round me, all was quiet, the sky was beautifully clear, and the southern stars were shining in all their glory.

CHAPTER VIII.

A HUNT IN CANOES.—AN ANTELOPE PURSUED.—I AM NEARLY CAPSIZED.—KILLING OF THE ANTELOPE.—RETURN TO THE VILLAGE.

THE palaver being settled to the great joy of every body, the people said I must leave to hunt with the dogs, as antelopes had been seen the last few days on the neighboring plantations. So, early in the morning, all the dogs of the village were collected together, and a number of hunters from other villages had also come with their dogs. We had altogether more than twenty dogs in the pack, and anticipated a very exciting time. The Apingi forming the hunting party were armed with spears. As soon as the party was ready, we set out for a plantation not far from the bank of a river or creek, which ran near the village, and where antelopes were supposed to be quite plentiful. The little canoes of the Apingi were in readiness, with paddles in, at different places on the river bank, for it was supposed that some of the antelopes would be driven into the water by the dogs.

So we started, Remandji and the villagers wishing us good luck. We tramped away through the jungle, and in less than an hour reached a plantation of cassada (manioc), the leaves of which antelopes and gazelles are very fond of. This plantation was not far from the river.

The dogs started off, and soon we heard them barking. The barking became loud and eager; it came nearer and nearer, and we knew the dogs must be after an antelope. They were evidently making toward the river, near which our party was posted. There was no time to be lost. We must hurry to the river side, and enter the canoe, to be ready in case the animal should plunge into the water to escape to the other side. I tell you, we went double-quick. Hollo! hollo! a cry of pain escaped from me, for the prickly branches of a long, thorny brier were round my leg. In my eagerness to go fast, I did not perceive it until it tore my pantaloons, and some of the thorns stuck into my legs. At last I got clear of it and hurried on. Okabi followed me closely. We soon came to the banks of the river. A superb antelope, with a magnificent pair of horns, was already in the water, and the infuriated dogs were after her. The last of the pack were just plunging in, and those that were in the water were swimming as fast as they could in pursuit. Three canoes were already in the water, the Apingi paddling as fast as they could toward the antelope. I jumped into a canoe with Okabi so impatiently that I almost lost my equilibrium. The canoe rocked from side to side, and for a moment I thought it was all over with me, and that I was going to be upset, gun and all, into the water, which, by the way, was very deep there. Then good-by to my hunting for that day. Okabi uttered a loud cry, in the hope, I suppose, of averting the danger. But the little canoe became steady once more, and I seated myself on the bottom. It was an old affair, and leaked like an old basket, and having no seat, I got very uncomfortably wet. Never mind, I thought, the antelope is ahead of us. "Hurry, Okabi!" I shouted. "Hurry up! we must catch the antelope! We must kill it; we must carry off the honors of the hunt!" Okabi did not need any pushing; he felt exactly as I did, and we both paddled with all our strength. Three spears lay ready at the bottom of the canoe by my side. The chase became more and more exciting; nearer and nearer we came to the antelope. We soon passed one canoe, but two were still ahead of us, and these were not far from the antelope. "Hurry, Okabi!" I shouted. The fellow paddled as if his life was at stake, and by this time was covered with perspiration. We at last passed the two canoes. We were ahead of every body. The antelope, which had been carried by the current down the river, was nearing the shore. As soon as we were near enough, I cried out to Okabi to stop. He obeyed, steadying the canoe with his paddle. I took up my gun, and aimed at the antelope. There was danger that, if I missed it, I might kill one of the dogs. I took my chance, and fired. The ball hit the antelope in the right place, and the water was reddened with its blood. I fired again, but the canoe rocked a little just as I pulled the trigger, and the ball missed the mark. By this time the antelope had struggled to land, but as it came out of the water it dropped dead on the bank. The excited dogs sprang barking about the body, and we had the greatest trouble to drive them away.

We returned to the village, where we were welcomed with shouts of joy. I took a hind quarter for my share, and gave the rest to Remandji to divide among his people.

CHAPTER IX.

BEAUTIFUL SIGHT OF PALM-TREES.—HOW PALM-OIL IS MANUFACTURED.—ITS VALUE.—INDIA-RUBBER VINES.—A LEOPARD.—HE IS TRACKED.—TERRIBLE SUSPENSE.—THE LEOPARD IS KILLED.

THE people had learned that I wanted no war, and promised to remain peaceful. I left the village the next day, and continued my journey through the jungle, visiting the Apingi villages, and at the same time studying the natural resources of the country, the crowd accompanying me increasing all the time as I passed village after village. We came at length to a village surrounded with immense groves of palm-trees, which, indeed, were scattered all over the forest in great numbers. These palm-trees were covered with large bunches of yellow nuts, from which palm-oil is derived, which forms, perhaps, the most important article of trade on the west coast of Africa. Knowing it to be very abundant, I concluded that a good trade in palm-oil could be made with the Coast, and that, if it was conducted on the right principle, and not by exchanging oil for rum, the Apingi would do very well. So I fixed my head-quarters in a village where the manufacture of palm-oil was carried on on a large scale, the inhabitants selling it to the people of all the other villages. It is used very extensively among the Africans. Every woman in a village must have a little calabash of palm-oil to make her toilet with. They rub their bodies with it, it is used as a kind of pomade for their hair, and they use it as we do butter in food. I can assure you that the heads of these people do not smell very agreeably, as they never wash, while they keep putting palm-oil on their hair day after day, month after month, year after year; the fragrance is any thing but delightful.

I was much pleased to see these people industrious in the manufacture of palm-oil. Perhaps you would like to have a description of the town where this manufacture was carried on. You must not expect to hear about huge smoking chimneys, tall buildings with a great number of windows, and a great many men and women at work.

How beautiful is the sight of these palm-trees! How tall and graceful they are, and how splendid their fruit looks! The palm-trees about the village were kept very carefully, and were never destroyed, for every year they bore fruits which brought a great revenue to the village. The forest was filled with knots of women seated on the ground, who had clubbed together for the manufacture of the oil. After it had been manufactured they divided the proceeds.

Each little company was very busy. There would be seated women having three or four large earthenware cooking-pots filled up with palm-oil nuts, which they were boiling. After being thoroughly boiled, these were given to other women, who had before them a large wooden mortar some five or six feet long, about twelve or eighteen inches broad, and a foot deep, made of a single piece of wood. The boiled nuts were put into

these mortars, and pounded by the women with heavy pestles made of the hardest kind of wood. The palm-oil nut has a very large and heavy kernel, of the size of our walnuts, which is very thick, and exceedingly hard, so much so that I doubt very much, though I have never tried it, whether a nut-cracker could break it. The kernel is covered with a fibrous pulp, which is about the fourth or fifth part of an inch thick, and which is almost literally made of oil. It is hard, but

MAKING PALM-OIL.

when the nut is boiled becomes soft. The nuts grow in large bunches, and each palm-tree bears several of these bunches. They grow near the trunk, where the branches spring out; and the nuts are very close together, several hundred of them growing in a single bunch.

These nuts at first are blackish, then, as they ripen, and especially on the side toward the sun, become of a bright yellow, from which the palm-oil derives its color.

After the nuts have been boiled and pounded, the oil is put into another cooking-pot, and then put over the fire, and the oil allowed to boil for a little while. They then let it rest and cool, and then carefully pour it out, taking great care not to disturb the dregs at the bottom, which is chiefly composed of the fibres of the nuts. Then the oil is put carefully in little calabashes and carried to market.

The men take but a small share in the work. They have only to climb the trees, and cut off the bunches, and bring them to the women. The nuts are picked from the bunches before boiling. Before they have attained their full growth, these nuts have thorny points at the end. They are not round, and not even in size or shape, on account of being pressed against each other closely while growing in the bunches.

It was pleasant to see these people hard at work, and I had a real nice time with them. When night came on I slept in the midst of them; and one of the men came and kindly presented me with two fat rats for my dinner.

But I could see at a glance how little the African trade could be increased. Here was a region that could have little or no trade whatever with the Coast, for there were too many tribes between it and the sea.

How cheap was the oil! A few beads would buy a gallon of it. A factory established here could do a large if not very profitable business, and in course of time more ready intercourse might be established with the Coast. The business, once set on foot, would require but little care. The trees bear every year, and the only thing to be done would be to gather the nuts and make the oil in the manner I have described.

Palm-oil has always a ready sale in civilized countries. It is used extensively in the manufacture of soap, candles, and in some countries of Europe it is used instead of tallow to grease railway and carriage wheels, and machinery.

I forgot to mention that there is in the kernel of the palm-nut a large seed, from which a great quantity of oil can be extracted.

The next morning, before my departure, I received presents of many calabashes of oil.

In proceeding to another village I saw what I had noticed before, that the whole forest was filled with India-rubber vines. As the vines are very plentiful in these forests, an enormous quantity of India-rubber could be extracted from them in the manner which I have already described to you in Stories of the Gorilla Country. This might be made a large trade. The India-rubber could be bought for next to nothing, and the profits would be enormous, and a good market could be found. So here were two productions which the Apingi could collect in great quantities. There were also immense numbers of ebony-trees, the wood of which is so beautiful, and which could be exported in large quantities, if we could only have a free road to the Coast.

That night we were to sleep in the forest; so, before sunset, we built a large camp for shelter. But there was no sleep for me; the leopards were too plentiful, and their dismal and ferocious howls resounding not far from the camp told me that we had better keep a bright look-out. I forbade any one to move out of the light of the fires during the night; but there was little need of the caution, as they knew very well that if they did they would never come back to the camp. The next day I proposed a leopard-hunt. The next morning, when I got up, and said we must find the lair of the leopard, the people seemed to back down; but I was not willing to give it up, as the leopards were evidently not far from us, and their lair must be near by. I wanted only four Apingi to go with me.

So I called four of the warriors. I gave two guns to them, and one preferred to go with his war spears.

After a while we came to the bank of a little stream, where I discovered the footprints of a huge leopard in the soft ground. What paws! It must be an old and ferocious animal. I have not the slightest doubt that the monster was an old fellow, and that it was the one that came so near our camp during the night, and nothing but the big fires we kept up had frightened him away and prevented him from pouncing upon us. Unless the leopard had caught something last night he must be fearfully hungry, and, consequently, very fierce. I must look out, for, in that case, if I see him I will have but very little time to fire, for in a jiffy he will spring upon me, said I to myself.

So I carefully followed along the banks of the stream the footprints of the huge cat. If he sees me first he may pounce upon me, as a cat does upon a mouse. I must be careful. The Apingi are watchful. They look all round; their ears are ready to hear the least noise. All at once I hear a cluck from one of the men. I stop; he points out to me a spot ahead, just by the stream, where the underbrush or jungle is very thick. Huge trees have fallen one upon another, and it is impossible to see through the mass. The leopard must be there. This dark place must be his abode for the day. There he hides himself and sleeps, and from there he starts upon his depredations, spreading fear and terror among beasts and men. I stand ready to fire at a second's notice. I wish you could have seen me. I knew that it was a matter of life and death with me. I follow the track of the leopard, for it had walked all along the little stream. The Apingi men are not mistaken. Suddenly the footprints leave the river, and the last I see of them show that the animal has retired into that thick, dark, and almost impenetrable part of the jungle where the Apingi had told me that the leopard was concealed. This is dangerous game. I can not see the enemy. It is dangerous to go in. I can not back out; I dare not show the Apingi that I am afraid. But then I do not wish to be killed by an infuriated leopard.

The best thing I can do is to use caution as I enter the thicket. The Apingi are almost afraid to go in. But we must do it. I lead. Oh, I wish I had some native dogs with me; they would bark and show us the lair of the leopard. After a while I succeeded in climbing to the top of the huge tree that had been blown down by a tornado. It is at least ten feet in diameter. When once lodged there I take a view of the surroundings.

The Apingi are close at my back. They are evidently afraid, and, for myself, I do not feel very comfortable, for you will agree with me that it is a difficult position to be in, not to see the exact location of such a dangerous enemy as the leopard, which at any moment might be down on my back, his claws fastened in my shoulders, and his big teeth in my neck. Such thoughts were not very reassuring to a worn traveler.

I must confess that I was very much excited. I looked round and round. The slightest noise made by the wind through the trees would startle me. I thought the leopard was close at hand and ready to spring upon me. I would have given a good deal to see him. Carefully I came down the trunk of the huge tree, and continued to press forward with my Apingi into the thickest part of this already very thick jungle.

Suddenly the faces of my Apingi men become excited. They stop walking. The strong odor of the leopard is clearly perceptible: he is evidently not far from us. We are upon the leopard, and he is probably eying us, and ready to make a spring. We must hurry to see him, for surely destruction is coming upon us unless we destroy the animal. I look ahead into a thick bush, where were a large number of broken branches. It seems almost dark, though it is not noon yet, and the sky is clear, and the sun shines resplendently. Every thing round is in gloom. A cold shiver runs through me. A feeling of insecurity begins to possess me. I must check it, for, if I do not, my arm will not be steady, and I shall miss the monster if I see him. The thought of home and friends rushed to my mind. The feeling of insecurity suddenly disappeared. I must conquer this big wild cat of the forest. If he is wary, I too must be wary.

Whew! hallo! I see the monster! He is lying on the dead branch of a tree. He leaps upon the ground and crouches upon it. His long tail wags to and fro, showing that he is enraged. His eyes glisten with a singular light; he is ready to spring. He springs, but, just as his body seems to rise from the ground, a tremendous and deadly steel-pointed bullet goes through his head, and three spears of the Apingi are plunged into his body. The monster rolls on the ground upon his back, uttering fearful yells of pain that fill the forest, and drive every living animal from the neighborhood. By this time my breath is taken away. I am so excited that my heart beats with fearful quickness. I must be pale as death, for the excitement is great; for, one second more, and the monster would have made its deadly spring, which would have been destruction to me.

I was glad when the chase was over, and I concluded that I would rather chase the leopard at night with a goat tied to a tree for a lure; but then I must not do as I did once before—fall asleep with the goat—as I have previously described to you, for, perhaps, instead of taking the goat, it might take me.

When we got back to the camp there was an immense excitement. The Apingi said that they had killed the leopard also, for three of their spears had been in his body. It was a huge old fellow. I wish you could have seen his teeth and his large paws. What tremendous claws it had! With a blow of his paw the monster could have killed the strongest man.

I was greatly pleased to secure this animal, for its skin

was superb, and I knew that I would gladden the heart of some friend at home when I should present it to him.

Here, again, more cooks were to be fastened on me, the people insisting that twenty of their women should follow Remandji and myself. With my old housekeeper, and the forty-three cooks, I had now sixty-four cooks.

LAIR OF THE LEOPARD.

CHAPTER X.

MANUFACTURE OF POTTERY.—NUMEROUS COOKS.—PLANTAIN PLANTATIONS.

THE next morning I started again on my journey, and visited a good many small Apingi villages. At length I came to one where the manufacture of earthenware was carried on extensively by the people. Cooking utensils and water-jars were made in great numbers with a kind of grayish clay. Pipes were also manufactured, for I must tell you that the Apingi cultivate tobacco extensively in their country, and are very much given to smoking.

The people of the village had seen me at Remandji's, and were not afraid. I had hardly entered the village when the good chief came to meet me with thirteen women, and courteously insisted that I should take them for wives and cooks. Of course I declined, but the chief insisted that they should follow me, with the other sixty-four, wherever I traveled in the Apingi country.

The way these simple people worked their pottery was very primitive. They would work and pound the clay till it was thoroughly mixed, and every particle of it very fine. Then they would mould it into the shape of the vases or pots they wanted to have, and, when these had been fashioned and finished exactly as they wished, they would put them in the shade under a veranda or shed. When hardened a little they are gradually exposed to the sun till they are quite hard, and then they are baked over a fire. I give you the shape of these vases in the annexed engraving. I found that among all the tribes they were of the same shape. The cannibals made pottery exactly as these Apingi.

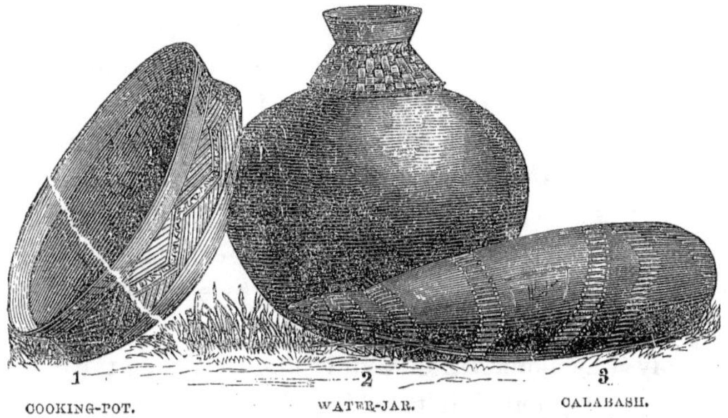

COOKING-POT. WATER-JAR. CALABASH.

The large water-jugs are the most difficult to manufacture, and are rather fragile. They have to make a frame of wicker-work, upon which they lay the clay. Calabashes are used extensively for water-vessels.

I was pleased to find that many of the Apingi villages had remained long at the same place; for the Apingi, unlike almost all the tribes that surround them, do not feel the necessity of moving their village after a death or two. The people would show me trees bearing berries or fruits in the shape of an olive, which had often been planted by their fathers, or by themselves when young. So ovation after ovation kept following me as I came to village after village. I was a real king, and was treated as such. Feast after feast was given me by the chiefs, and such queer bills of fare as we had! Such dainties as came upon the table! Why, there were mice, rats, squir-

D

rels, monkeys, snakes, turtles, fish, eels, hyena, etc.; but not one of them could give me such a feast as good old Obindji had given to me and to my powerful friend King Quengueza.

I do not know why, but every day in that far Apingi country I loved to think of good old Quengueza. I loved to think of Gambo, of Malaouen, and of poor Querlaouen. Poor Querlaouen, how much I miss him since his death! I can hardly believe that he is no more. How brave he was! This you know as well as I do. What a kind heart God had given to his poor savage nature! But you will no more read of our hunting together when I return to his country.

On my way home, after a few more days of travel in my new kingdom, I felt tired as I came in the evening to a large plantation where there was an innumerable number of plantain-trees, and a great many bore immense bunches. The plantain bunch is much like that of the banana, and ripens like it by turning yellow or red, according to the variety. It is much larger than the banana, coarser, very sweet when ripe, and delightful eating when roasted. There are a great number of varieties of plantain, far more so than of banana. Some of the trees bear after six or eight months, others take a year, some a year and a half. There are varieties that bear prodigious bunches, weighing from one hundred to one hundred and fifty pounds. In the interior they flourish splendidly, and now and then you see bunches much heavier than one hundred and fifty pounds.

Now I will explain to you how the best plantain plantations are made, and you will see that there is no other species of food that can be raised in such a quantity on so small a lot of land.

Of course you are aware that the banana and plantain trees, with few exceptions, bear only a single bunch, and then die. The varieties that bear the quickest have the smallest bunches. A great many of these weigh only from twenty to twenty-five pounds, and sometimes even less. But judge of the quantity of food which an acre of ground can bear when planted with the varieties of trees that bear the heaviest bunches. A plantation is stocked with the shoots of the plantain-tree. The plantain shoots are set out about six feet apart, and sometimes more. Other shoots spring from them—sometimes as many as six or eight before the tree has done bearing and dies. Each of these shoots become trees themselves, and bear; a few of these are retransplanted, in order to give the others more room to grow.

The shade of plantain-trees, after they have grown to a certain height, prevents every kind of weeds from growing under them; hence, after a plantation has been started well—that is to say, that the young plantain-trees have grown healthy and strong, and the foliage has become thick, it requires no care at all.

Now let us say that six square feet of land will give six plantain-trees, which bear six bunches of plantains within two years. If the plantains belong to the heavy-bunch variety, these will weigh about from eighty to one hundred and twenty pounds—to make an average, we will say one hundred pounds. So in two years six hundred pounds of food have been produced on six square feet of land. But then the weight of the skin and of the stem must be deducted, and the average weight of these is a third of the gross weight. All the calculations I made did bear that proportion.

So food to the amount of four hundred pounds is raised on six feet square of land in two years, or at an average of two hundred pounds of food a year; so I think we may safely say that the plantain-tree gives more food to the human race in proportion to space than any other plant.

The natives eat the plantain green. It is then tasteless, and when coming out of the boiling pot it is very mellow and quite palatable when once accustomed to it.

Nothing is more beautiful than a cluster of plantain-trees protected by the forest from the winds; the immense leaves, some of them over eight feet long, make a superb appearance.

In despite of all this luxuriance, the negroes are at times straitened for food, for the plantains, unlike grain, do not keep long after being picked from the tree in that hot climate. In four or five days after they have been cut they begin to be too ripe to eat, and rot very soon after. So, if your plantation bears more than you want, you must give them away, for there is no market in that part of the world, no real starving people, no poor, for these people, though not Christians, never allow a stranger to be hungry.

The land for a new plantation is cleared in the following manner: The trees of the forest are cut down in the dry season; then, after a while, fire is set to them, and afterward the young plantain-trees are transplanted in the midst of the numberless trunks and limbs of trees that the fire had not been able to destroy.

CHAPTER XI.

THE KENDO.—ITS SMALL SIZE.—I KILL ONE.—ASTONISHMENT OF THE NATIVES.

On my way back to Remandji I saw a good many little squirrels in that great African forest; but there is one little fellow so very small and tiny that I am sure it must be the smallest squirrel in the world. I must tell you something about it. The natives called it kendo. It was entirely a new species to me. Being so small, I called it *Sciurus minutus* when I gave a description of it in the Proceedings of the Boston Society of Natural History for 1860, p. 366. I remember the first time I met a kendo I was with my great friend Querlaouen, just by a swamp, hidden and watching for wild ducks that were in the habit of coming to it every day. All at once I saw climbing along the trunk of a tree a little animal, which seemed so small that I had some doubt about my having seen any thing at all. I lost sight of it in a few seconds, then got sight of it again, but only for a second, as I hardly had my eye upon it when it vanished. Querlaouen saw it also, and told me it was a kendo. I immediately drew the heavy charge from one of the barrels of my gun and reloaded with the smallest kind of shot I had, and which was used by me to kill very small birds.

At last I got sight again of a little kendo. He was gnawing a little bit of the bark of the tree, and was

THE SCIURUS MINUTUS, OR KENDO.

standing still. It was the most graceful little tiny thing I had seen. Just as I raised my gun he moved away, but as quickly as possible I followed him in his movement, and as soon as I saw a good chance I fired, and the poor little thing tumbled down to the ground, to the utter amazement of friend Querlaouen, who was sure that I had a big monda (fetich) to be able to hit such a little thing. During my sojourn in Africa I killed several more of these little kendos, and brought their stuffed skins back, and as I know that you would like to see just how big the little animal is, there stands before you a picture of a full grown specimen.

I can not tell you the astonishment of Remandji when he saw I had been successful in killing the kendo. I was in his eye a much greater spirit than ever; so, if Querlaouen was astonished, you must just fancy how much more amazed Remandji was.

The next day we got back to Remandji, where every demonstration of joy from the villagers welcomed us. I entered the village with a very large retinue of women as cooks, headed, of course, by my old housekeeper, who insisted on taking the lead and being first in every thing, because, as she said, she was the first that had been given to me. I gave to each of these poor creatures a few big beads, and then dismissed them, and they returned to their own villages feeling quite happy.

Wandering the next morning in the forest with Okabi, I heard a very strange sound, and stopped to listen and find out what it was.

CHAPTER XII.

A HERD OF MONKEYS.—HOW THEY TRAVEL IN THE FOREST. —WHITE-NOSED MONKEYS.—THEIR GREAT LEAPS.—HOW THEY KEEP FOOD WHEN NOT HUNGRY.

"Hark!" said I, "hark! What is the noise I hear? It must come from a band of monkeys traveling in the forest from tree to tree. It is no use to go to them," said I to Okabi; "let us hide ourselves in the direction where the noise comes from, and if they come in a straight line they may pass over our heads, and we may then have a good shot at them." This was hardly said before it was done. We hid ourselves under a thick little bush. The noise came nearer and nearer. Ho! ho! I thought, they are going to pass just over our heads. This was a great piece of good fortune.

I hid myself the best way I could, squatting close to the ground, and sinking my neck into my shoulders as much as possible, and hardly dared to breathe, when, by jingo, I felt like sneezing! It would have been nice work to sneeze just when the monkeys were close by, and to frighten them away, for the monkeys are shy here, being much hunted by the natives. Many and many hundreds of them have met their death by the arrows and traps of the skillful hunters. But here they come! I see the branches at the top of the trees moving. There must be at least fifteen or twenty monkeys, belonging to the white-nosed tribe, upon a journey. It was marvelous to see them seize the branches and swing themselves, in order to leap farther, just like a man on a trapeze. As they came down to the extremity of the light branches, these would bend several feet under their weight. They would leap to another branch, seize one, and then to another, never stopping to rest. Sometimes they would run a few steps on some long and stout branch, and leap again. In some places where the trees were not very near together in the direction in which they wished to travel, they would take flying leaps of fifteen to twenty feet, straight through the air, from branch to branch, without stopping to measure the distance. I was so deeply interested in watching their movements that I quite forgot that I had a gun, and that I was hungry. One by one they passed on, flying along like as if they had wings, or by magic, reaching the branch they aimed at with unerring certainty. Not one of them made a mistake; not one of them fell short of the branch he was after. In this manner monkeys journey for miles through the woods. Sometimes they make tremendous jumps from the upper boughs of high trees down to lower ones. I do not exaggerate at all when I say that sometimes I have surprised monkeys on high trees, and, after firing at them, I have seen them fall, apparently taking no heed, to a distance of thirty, forty, and perhaps fifty feet below, and disappear in the twinkling of an eye. Unless the monkeys shriek, there is no way to discover that they are about in the woods except by the noise occasioned by their tremendous leaps when on a journey, which sounds very strangely in the silence of these equatorial forests. On they go, leap after leap, for hours without resting. At other times, when they are only on a feeding excursion, and have reached a place where berries are abundant on the trees, they take it easy, and make their leaps slowly as they go along. It is by this noise chiefly that the hunters are guided when on the look-out for them. When there are many of them together they are difficult to approach, as they always have a sentinel on the watch, and at the least noise they decamp as fast as they can go; but when only two, three, or four of them are together, they are easier to approach, especially if they are hungry.

The white-nosed monkey, the ndova, and the white-mustached monkey, the "miengai," are tremendous leapers in those forests. I doubt very much whether the nkago ("cercocebus") is quite as good a leaper as the two others. They attain all of them to a very large size in the wild state, and a good many must weigh more than thirty or forty-five pounds. The enormous canines the big ones possess show what they can do in the way of biting.

I think that to see one of these flocks of monkeys on the march is one of the most interesting sights that ever gladdened my eyes in the great jungles of Africa. It is certainly a wonderful spectacle, for they seem to continue their flight without cessation, and without heeding what is before them. Their sight is so quick and keen, and their motion so rapid, that, on this occasion, I was unable to get within shot of them again after coming to my wits. It was a pleasure to watch them. So expert are they in their motions that they can stop at will, taking a firm grasp of the branch with the hind feet. The

MONKEYS JOURNEYING IN THE FOREST.

fore feet are only used in leaps to catch the branches toward which they spring.

Each of these three species of monkey has a very peculiar and distinct voice, the nkago having the most powerful. How often I have heard them, I should think almost a mile off, either calling for their absent mate, or, like other wild beasts, doing it merely for the pleasure of trying the strength of their lungs.

The cercopitheci and the cercocebi have very large pouches, which possess great power of distension, and they use them as store-houses, where they keep their nuts and berries when not hungry.

CHAPTER XIII.

ELEPHANT HUNTING. — TAKE REFUGE ON A TREE. — FIRE TWICE AT THE ELEPHANT.—HOW HE KICKED!—AN IMMENSE PYTHON.—HE KILLS ONE OF OUR DOGS.—OKABI KILLS THE SNAKE.

I HEAR that elephants are plentiful, and their heavy footprints are seen in a great many places in the forest. Antelopes and wild boars are also plentiful. I must have a peep at the elephants. I must go after them in the forest. I must kill one. Now is the time, for I know that a herd is in the forest, and, to judge by the natives pointing to the height of the sun to show the time we should find them if we start early in the morning at sunrise, I suppose that they must be about a four hours' walk from the village.

I have taken my best rifle; I have loaded it with steel-pointed bullets; I give to each of the two Apingi who are to accompany me a spare gun to carry, take food for the day, and we start.

After a while we came to fresh footprints, which evidently had been made where we were the day before; we followed their tracks. It was easy, for there must have been a herd of ten or twelve together. Oh how I wished I had one of my Bakalai friends with me, as we might have killed several elephants. We continued to follow the tracks, being careful, from time to time, to break a bough of a young tree, and drop on the ground a handful of green twigs, so as to make sure that we could find the way back again.

At last I thought I heard a noise, and gave a kind of cluck to stop my two Apingi friends, and raised my finger to my mouth to insure silence. There was no mistake. I could hear a booming sound, as if it was the heavy trampling of elephants. We advanced carefully. I could feel my heart beating violently, and I could almost hear its pulsations. These African elephants are ugly customers. The nimblest and coolest hunter is sometimes caught by them. Had not my splendid friend Querlaouen been killed by an elephant? Poor fellow! I had been thinking of him these last two hours. I often think of him. I thought also of friend Aboko, and wondered where he was. Perhaps he has been sold, said I to myself, or he may have been killed for witchcraft. Some of you may perhaps remember that Aboko was a great elephant hunter.

Such were my thoughts as I advanced into the jungle to meet the elephants. How lightly I stepped on the ground, for fear of making a noise and alarming the huge beasts!

I must remain still, for I discover that the elephants are retracing their steps; they are coming back by the same road. What does this mean? They are certainly unaware of our being so close to them. My friends the Apingi begin to show fear, and make me a sign that they are going to ascend a tree. They had hardly made the sign than they had climbed a pretty large tree, getting up among the lianes which hung from its branches. They were about twenty feet from the ground, resting on a heavy limb, and looked in the direction where we heard the noise.

Looking round, I saw close to them a nice tree, with a very thick trunk, just near the path the elephants had made by trampling the young saplings down. How to get up? Suddenly I saw a heavy liane, or creeper, hanging down from one of its branches. I slung my gun on my shoulder, seized the liane, and soon found myself some twenty feet up, between two immense limbs which diverged from the trunk. I stood between them, resting my back on one of the limbs. I was just in a right position if the elephants were to come back by the same path they had made. The noise becomes greater; they break down young trees as they advance, to eat their leaves. I hear their footsteps distinctly. They are coming by the same road.

I keep a sharp look-out through the dense foliage. The young trees begin to move, and I know that the elephants are near. The bull is in sight. I count nine elephants. The bull suddenly stops, sniffs the air, and elevates his trunk. He has smelt danger, no doubt. Oh dear! I can not aim well on account of being too high. I am sorry. I wish I had remained on the ground.

I shoulder my rifle. I aim at the bull, wishing to shoot him through the ear. I take good aim—bang! As ill luck would have it, just as I touched the trigger my foot slipped, and the bullet struck the elephant in the head, wounding him badly, but not killing him. He immediately charges on the tree, when suddenly he perceives my two Apingi friends, and makes a rush for their tree, tearing down the vines which hang from it. I fire again, and the ball hits him on the hip. He gives a tremendous kick, raises his hind legs up, and plunges into the forest with fearful noise, tearing every thing that opposed him, and leaving tracks of blood behind. I was happy to see the last of him, as I did not feel at home on the tree. If I had been on the ground I would have probably killed him. The other elephants, when they heard the first gun, dashed into the forest at a fearful speed, demolishing every thing before them. When the Apingi came down from their tree, they looked almost dead with fright. I was not satisfied with myself, for I wished I had "bagged" the elephant.

I came down from my place of concealment, and for the remainder of the day went after the other elephants; but they had fled far away, and I was at length obliged to give up the chase. We made our camp that night in the woods. I lighted a fire without trouble. We made a nice shelter with leaves, for we had rain almost every night; and, surrounded by bright fires, we lay down to sleep. The leopards were prowling about, so we did not all dare to sleep at once. One must keep watch, and see that the fires were bright. We had no trouble in doing this, as we had collected a great quantity of fire-wood.

The next morning we returned to Remandji. My two Apingi told marvelous stories about my gun, and what a kicking the elephant made when he received a bullet in his hind quarter. Every one laughed heartily, and some of the villagers prepared to go into the forest to hunt for the wounded elephant, for they say he has surely died. I should not wonder if he should be found dead somewhere in the jungle in a few days.

The following day I went hunting again. Okabi was my only companion. Okabi had taken with him four of his dogs, and we had great hopes of killing some wild boars. Suddenly the dogs, which were running in the forest, appeared excited, as if they were on the track of game, and the four were soon out of sight. Soon afterward we heard them barking, which at last became less and less distinct, till the sound was entirely lost. "Yes," said I to Okabi, "there must be game in the forest; what can it be?" "I can not tell," said Okabi. I fully expected to hear the barking of the dogs come once more toward us, for these dogs were so trained as to drive the game in the direction of the hunters. We were not mistaken. A little after we heard the barking of the dogs, but once more it gradually grew fainter and fainter, and all became silent. Okabi shouted all the time in Apingi to the dogs to come back, so that they might know the direction in which we were. All continued silent. We waited for an hour; the same silence still prevailed, and we concluded that the game had been fleeter than the dogs, and had given them the slip. It might have been an antelope, and perhaps it had crossed some stream; but then these native dogs are not afraid of water, and they would have gone in pursuit. Perhaps it might have been a chimpanzee. In fact, we did not know what game it was, and Okabi and I wished we knew.

The dogs are at last coming back. We hear their footsteps in the jungle, and now one is in sight. But hark! I hear a howl of pain from one of them, as if it had been seized by a wild beast. We are on the *qui vive.* I cock my gun. Who knows but that there may be a gorilla close by, or perhaps a fierce leopard has sprung upon the dog. It may be a wild beast with which I have never been acquainted. But never mind; I am ready; my gun is loaded for big game. I look round. The three dogs bark, and I cautiously go in their direction. What meets my eyes? An immense python, that had been lying in wait by a little rivulet, coiled round a tree, no doubt waiting for some gazelle or other game to come and drink, had sprung and coiled itself round the poor dog, and was drawing itself tighter and tighter round his body. I rush forward with Okabi. The snake at the same time had seen us, and seemed, to all appearances, not to know what to do. I did not like to fire, lest I should kill the poor dog that was struggling in its folds. Okabi, taking the cutlass he had by his side, goes to the rescue, and cuts the body of the snake in two. The iron grip of his fold gives way, and the dog, appearing half dead, lies prostrate on the ground. It had been almost squeezed to death. The two parts of the body of the big python, or huge African boa, still quivered and wriggled almost as if it was still alive. One blow more from Okabi's cutlass, and one half is divided in two again, and with the butt-end of my gun I smash his head.

We were too busy with the snake first to look after the dog; but, after killing the reptile, we came to poor doggy. I took him to the border of the little rivulet, and sprinkled him with water, in order to see if we could not revive him. But all we did was of no avail. He had been squeezed too long (though but a short time) in the folds of the snake. In a second or two his eyes became dim, and after a few struggles of the limbs and gasps for breath, the poor dog died. Okabi was furious, for it was a trained dog. We took with us the snake, which measured fifteen feet in length.

CHAPTER XIV.

SERIOUS THOUGHTS.—SHALL I REMAIN TO BE THEIR KING?—WILL THE APINGI FIGHT?—I MUST RAISE A REVENUE.—PRODUCTS OF THE COUNTRY.

I MUST begin to think seriously of what can be done for the improvement of my kingdom. Did the people really believe that I was to remain with them forever? Of course they never dreamed that I could die. I had not made up my mind how long I would remain, for I had a strong desire to go back to the sea-shore and return to New York.

Then I thought how strange it would be if I staid with them till the end of my days! If such was the case, said I to myself, I must establish communication with the sea-shore, first by means of the big river, and then by land. But the Rembo-Apingi (Rembo meaning the river) was a large stream, and numerous tribes were living on its banks. Some of them were very warlike, and there had never been communication from the Apingi to the mouth of the Fernand Vaz. From Remandji's village to my settlement of Washington there was a great extent of country to go through. There would be, no doubt, some tremendous fighting to be done, for I knew enough of the country to know that the right of way was not to be obtained easily, each tribe being jealous of the other. Would the Apingi be willing to fight, and conquer or die? In that case I must go once more to the sea-coast, bring small cannon, quantities of guns, pistols, and every thing required to make us formidable, so that we might be feared by all the tribes in case they should try to prevent us from having communication with the sea. Large canoes also must be made, capable of holding at least one hundred warriors, for I must have a powerful navy to navigate the river. The men must be taught how to use guns, how to fire, and, above all, not to shrink from danger.

I began to see that I had a gigantic task before me. Of course I did not intend to be a king of savages. I wanted the people to advance in civilization. Schools must be established. The people must learn how to read and write. They must be taught by all means, so that in the course of time, from their own free will (for I believe in liberty of conscience), they might destroy their idols, cast away their superstitions, and believe in God as the great Ruler of the universe. They must admit the good missionaries, who could instruct them in his worship.

Then, again, every country must have a revenue. How shall I raise taxes? I can not raise money, for it is unknown here, and silver and gold have never been seen by the people. What were the products of the country? What could be got out of it? For no government can be carried on without a revenue of some kind. Palm-oil, India-rubber, ivory, ebony-wood, bar-wood, gum copal—these are the leading products of the country: great quantities of them could be had. A numerous fleet of canoes, constructed especially to carry goods, must be constructed. They must be very large, and strongly built. They could go down the river loaded with a few men in each, but they must be convoyed by powerful war-canoes, that could defy and destroy any hostile canoe that might come out against them.

Peace must reign along the borders of the river, from the Apingi country to its mouth. Laws must be strictly enforced and obeyed, and war between villages and tribes along the river must be forbidden, just as King Quengueza has forbidden war on the Ovenga River, and the refractory people must be punished, and their villages burnt, so that they may learn that no laws can be broken without cost. In fact, peace must reign every where in the country, so that commerce may be thrifty and the people happy.

These thoughts brought me back again to the question of a revenue.

How many tons of ebony, pounds of ivory, tons of palm-oil, and pounds of India-rubber would have to be collected by the people, in order to raise, for the first year, $100,000? Say—

10,000 lbs. of ivory, at $2 per lb.	$20,000
200 tons of palm-oil, at $200 per ton	40,000
1000 tons of ebony, at $100 per ton	100,000
10 tons of wax, at $650 per ton	6,500
100,000 lbs. of India-rubber, collected carefully, would be worth 20 cents per lb.	20,000
10 tons of gum copal, at $650 per ton	6,500

I could easily collect $182,000. As for the bar-wood, it is too far away, except if collected near the sea-shore, for it is only worth about $25 per ton. No doubt the trade could be increased vastly in a short time with the interior of Africa. I put the amount of each product according to the amount of production, that is to say, in ratio. I have no doubt that in time the palm-oil would become one of the leading products of the country. There are great quantities of pea-nuts in that region, and an immense amount of oil could be manufactured, if mills were established for that purpose. It is very easy of manufacture. The pea-nut yields an enormous quantity of oil—I think more than five eighths of its own weight. South from the Apingi, malachite and copper must be abundant, for they come to Loango from the interior. What a profitable branch of commerce this might be made! In many parts of the mountains very rich iron ore is plentiful; and, should it in time become civilized, there will be no trouble in building railways. The forests furnish an inexhaustible supply of timber. A species of teak is found near the sea-shore. Saw-mills could be erected to make all this available in time. I am fully persuaded that one of these days—it may be a very long time yet—we will have to come to Africa for timber. Then there must be precious stones in those rocky and woody mountains; and it is not improbable that gold may be found in sufficient abundance to pay well for mining. Unfortunately, no dependence could be placed on agricultural products, for no negro loves to cultivate the soil.

The social system, also, must be entirely reformed in this part of the world before agriculture can flourish. Men must be taught to cultivate the soil themselves instead of leaving it to their wives. You have seen, in reading the previous books of this series, that men do not work. Not one of them would like to go and cultivate the soil. They think it is beneath their dignity, and that it is for women only to handle the spade and hoe

You have seen that all the products I have spoken of, as furnishing means to raise a revenue, are native products. The one exception is the pea-nut, which, however, grows there, when planted, with great luxuriance.

I must also teach the natives to plant rice, so that they may have food that will keep. They never had seen rice before I came to their country, though in some parts of Africa the natives plant and live upon it. I must also make them plant Indian corn, as this is also food that will keep. I must tell you that Indian corn is often found among the tribes near the Coast, but the plant is gradually finding its way into the interior.

I thought I would let some time pass away before I made up my mind what I should do. If I conclude to remain to be their king, I must go home and get a wife. A smile came over me at that very thought, for it was the first time I had thought of the subject in my life. What a tremendous excitement there would be if I ever came to the Apingi country with a wife, especially if she had blue eyes, and long fair or flaxen hair hanging down over her shoulders! I am sure I would set the Apingi people crazy. They would certainly fall down and worship her as a beautiful and unknown spirit that had risen out of some clear and limpid stream which meanders through the forest.

CHAPTER XV.

I DISCOVER A GALAGO'S LAIR.—CAPTURE OF THE GALAGO.
—TWO BABY GALAGOS.

ONE afternoon, after thinking over all these things, I went all alone into the forest, for I was tired of the noise of the people, and wanted to reflect seriously upon my future movements. Suddenly, while walking slowly along, I came to the foot of a tree, which at once attracted my attention, so that I stopped to examine it. It was old, not very tall, but thick in the trunk, and full of knots. A great many dead branches of other trees had fallen upon it, and these were so thick that they prevented the light from penetrating below. It is upon such trees and in their hollows that night-animals generally retire for the day, for it is almost dark as night in its thick recesses. So, thinking that perhaps I should find some new species of night-animal hidden in such a collection of dead and broken limbs, I stooped, and tried to peer into that dense and tangled mass. First I tried to see if there were any snakes hidden there, for snakes are fond of such places. Not a snake could be seen; but then some of them are not discovered so easily, for they are of the same color as the dead branches, and among those which have this color there are some very venomous species. Nor could I discover any traces of wild cats.

Suddenly it struck me that just where the branches parted from the main trunk the bark seemed somewhat more shining, as if some little wild animal was in the habit of climbing every day to the same spot. I looked carefully in that direction, but nothing was to be seen. There must be, certainly, a hole in the tree, I thought. Just by that tree hung a big creeper, as big as a large rope, strong enough to hold the mast of a ship, and by climbing it I could just go up and get to the top of the tree. I felt that I must ascend; but, before doing it, I took again a sharp look, for I did not care at all to put my hand on a shining snake, or to have one drop down upon me. To make still more sure, I threw up a piece of wood into the thickest part of the branches. After waiting a little while, and seeing that nothing stirred, I prepared myself to ascend. My gun was bothering me. It seemed as if I could not possibly ascend with it, even after strapping it on my shoulder, and yet I did not care to leave it at the foot of the tree, for in these forests you have to look out sharp, as you do not know when your enemies may be near. It is true, I had my revolvers on my side, and, after some hesitation, I concluded to try, any how. The distance was not more than ten feet, and the thick rope of creepers made the ascent tolerably easy.

Before ascending, I looked all round to see that no savage was lurking near, and then began to climb up. It was rather hard work, after all, in despite of the support the thick creeper afforded me. I could not make up my mind to leave my gun behind, and it annoyed me a great deal by getting entangled in the branches, and my revolvers hung heavily from my belt; but I was bound to go up and see what was there. The hope of discovering some animal unknown to naturalists gave me strength to do things which in my ordinary moments I thought myself incapable of achieving.

At last I reached the forked part of the tree, and found I was not mistaken. A hollow was there, and by the appearance of the opening there was no doubt but that some little wild animal must make it its hiding-place.

Now came the rub. The idea of putting my hand inside of that dark hole was not very pleasant, for I did not know what kind of creature might be hiding there. No doubt it had four good canines which might go through my hands as if they were paper. I confess I did not relish the thought. How was it that I did not think of this before I ascended the tree? I was in a sad quandary, and did not know what to do. Now that I had reached the part of the tree where I wanted to be, after so much trouble, I did not care to go down and have taken the trouble for nothing; besides, who knew whether some pretty and unknown animal might not be hiding there? This last idea gave me courage, and I immediately sought in my head the best means either to capture or kill the animal. First I took from my belt one of my revolvers, and then looked down carefully into the hole to see if I could perceive the bottom of it, and thus discover what was there. Suddenly I perceived two big, bright red eyes, which seemed to send fire at me. It must be a galago, I thought. These little fellows have sharp little teeth, and can bite splendidly, and make you feel that they can hurt you. But I must try to capture instead of killing it, and then try to tame it and study its habits.

The hollow was only about fifteen inches deep. I was all alone, and I wished I had somebody with me, then we could have managed it more easily.

I immediately put my foot on the opening of the lair

of the galago so that he could not escape, then taking from the inside of my hat two pocket-handkerchiefs which I used to protect my head from the heat of the sun when I was under its rays, I put them round my hand, so that when I tied the little fellow fast his teeth would not go through.

Not far from me there was a little branch from which I could cut a nice little forked stick. Taking the big hunting-knife that hung in my belt, I cut the branch. It was just the thing I wanted. If I could put the fork on its neck, then I could with the other hand manage more safely the taking of the little fellow out of his lair, for no doubt he would make a desperate struggle.

So I took off my foot from the opening, and down went my forked stick; the little fellow whisked about in a lively manner, but soon he was caught, and began to cut up such capers with his hind legs, and tried so hard to get away, that I did not know if I should ever be able to handle it. But, putting my other arm down into the hole, I took a firm grip of the fellow by the neck, and I can assure you that I held him hard, for I had not much confidence in the wrapping of my hand, and I was dreadfully afraid I would get a bite from the little rascal, and be obliged to let go my hold. I got it safely out at last, though it made efforts to get away, and seized both of my shirt-sleeves with its little paws. But I held it firmly, and then perceived it was a female, and that she had young ones. Immediately I opened the bag where I kept my bullets, and in it I put the galago, and shut it again. Then once more I put in my hand, and soon brought up two very tiny little fellows. They were very pretty, with their soft, beautiful fur; but I was a little sorry they were so very young, as they would be harder to raise.

I descended the tree, delighted with my day's work, and started at once for the village with my capture. On arriving at home I immediately fixed a kind of cage, and put the galago and her young in it. This was merely a temporary arrangement, and my first care was to construct a permanent home for my new pets. Meanwhile I kept them in a box. Their house was quite ready for them the next day, and they seemed quite pleased with the change. I wanted especially to take great care of the little ones, in the hopes of taming them. But three days after their capture they died. The poor mother seemed very forlorn and lonely afterward. How forlorn her mate must have been when, on his return to the tree, he found his home deserted! He must have wandered all that night in search of her and of his young ones, or perhaps he knew at once that some perfidious enemy had despoiled his house.

Now all my hopes rested on the old one. For the first few days she would only eat at night, and her food was chiefly ripe plantains and bananas, and a few berries from the forest. Afterward she began to eat in the daytime, and would even take food from my hands. She was particularly fond of bananas. Then I made a little collar and put it round her neck, and tied her by a long string near my bed. She would keep awake the whole night, and make a desperate war on the roaches and other insects. The broad daylight seemed to hurt her eyes, and she would shut them up; but at night was quite another animal, and much more lively. One evening, by a very dim light, I watched her, and saw how quickly she would seize the roaches. She was so light-footed that she could not be heard.

Now I must give you a description of the galago. I must tell you that the animal possesses one of the softest furs I know. The natives use its skin to keep their powdered fetiches in. Its face is full of expression, the eyes being very large for the little head; the ears are almost transparent, the skin being very thin, stand upright, and are large for the size of the head. The eyes shine brightly, and during the day have a reddish appearance. Like all night-animals, they can see much better in the dark than in the daytime. The tail is somewhat bushy.

THE GALAGO.

The picture of a galago will give you an excellent idea of what the animal is like. A large specimen is of the size of a little puny cat.

The galago being a nocturnal animal, as soon as

darkness makes its appearance, it prepares itself to go out of its lair in search of food. It loves to feed upon insects, such as cockroaches, etc.; but, besides insects, it feeds on the fruits, berries, and nuts of the forest. Long before daylight it retires to its lair, and remains there during the whole day. It climbs about on trees from branch to branch like a monkey, and uses its fore feet like hands, as the monkey does, only it is far from being as agile as a monkey.

One fine morning I looked for the little galago, but she was not to be found. The string that held her had broken during the night, and she had *skedaddled* for parts unknown in the forest. I have often thought that if the galagos have a language of their own, my prisoner will have strange tales to tell of her captivity, and the only thing I could do after her flight was to wish that she might be happy once more in the woods, and that she might find her mate again.

CHAPTER XVI.

JACK, THE MONKEY. — HUNTING MONKEYS WITH DOGS. — GREAT FIGHT BETWEEN TWO DOGS AND A NKAGO.—CAPTURE OF A YOUNG NKAGO.—I GIVE HIM THE NAME OF JACK.

WHILE in the Apingi country, I had a queer little friend of which you have not heard yet. That friend was a little monkey which I had captured some time ago. It went by the name of Jack; or sometimes was called Jack Nkago, on account of his species being called Nkago by the natives. Jack was a dear little fellow, belonging to a family of monkeys called commonly by ourselves Mangabey, and, as he has been traveling with me for a long while, it has occurred to me that you would like to hear about him—how I captured him, how I raised him, and how I made a kind of civilized boy of him. Now let me tell you that Jack was a great friend of mine, and wherever I traveled he traveled also.

I must relate to you my first acquaintance with young Jack. One day that I felt very hungry while in the Apingi country, I started for a hunt in the woods, and I thought how nice it would be if I could kill a monkey. I had taken with me friend Okabi, with whom you are so well acquainted, and who is a good hunter; and, as we left the village, I said to Okabi, "I hope that we shall be able to kill a monkey." He replied at once, without any hesitation, "We shall be able to do so." "How do you know?" said I. "My monda (fetich) told me so," was his immediate answer.

Okabi took two of his queer little native hunting dogs with him, for it was a time of the year when monkeys frequently come down from the trees to pick up nuts and eat some kind of berries which, when ripe, fall on the ground. At first I was averse to taking the dogs with us, but they had been so well trained by friend Okabi in hunting dodges that I consented. One of these dogs was called, I remember, *Agounga*, and the other *Ipay*. Both of them were of rusty color, and had, like the rest of the breed that is found in that part of Africa, straight ears, a somewhat long muzzle, and when once on the hunting-path chasing game, were very swift in their movements. They were about three years of age, rather fierce, and afraid of hardly any thing excepting leopards. They would bark at a gorilla, but take good care to keep at a safe distance. These two dogs were always the first to attack the game, and, among their other exploits, had captured a young chimpanzee, several young wild boars, and a good many monkeys; Agounga showing, by several big scars, that the monkeys had often dealt badly with him, and that it required a good deal of pluck on his part to conquer, while Ipay's upper lip was on the side divided in two, showing what a tremendous bite an enormous monkey, of which he had got hold, gave him. Besides those two dogs, friend Okabi had four more, which, though not quite so cunning, were splendid hunting-dogs. They were descended from a family of dogs which had been for a long time celebrated as good hunters.

I can assure you that Agounga and Ipay were good

watch-dogs. No one could come on Okabi's plantation without their barking and raising "the Old Harry." It was a long time before I could accustom them to be friends with me, and I concluded that they could not bear the sight of a white man, as is often the case with dogs accustomed to African masters. I suppose that our American dogs that have never seen a black man would feel exactly the same in a reversed case. But after a good deal of patience, and plenty of meat and "good old bones" given to them by myself, I tamed them, and I was glad of it, for I did not care to have these dogs always after me when I made my appearance in Okabi's plantation, as I was always in dread that they would come and take a small piece of the calf of my leg. They are sly as can be, but, happily, mad dogs are entirely unknown in this part of the world, and I wonder sometimes if the introduction of our dogs will bring the dreadful disease of hydrophobia with it.

Now that I have given you an account of the dogs Agounga and Ipay, just follow me into the forest, and fancy that you can see us. Okabi was walking ahead in the hunting path with his gun in hand, and I was closely following him. The dogs were ahead of him about two or three yards. We had gone this way about two hours, when suddenly Okabi stopped, made a sign to the dogs to lie still, and then we listened attentively. Okabi's quick ear had detected a strange noise in the woods. I heard it also. The noise came incontestably from monkeys walking on the ground, for we could hear a rustling noise among the dead leaves as they moved amongst them and scattered them, to get the berries or nuts that had fallen underneath. There was no mistake.

The dogs were ordered silently to go forward, and it was time that they should do so, for they were almost ready to bark. They also had heard the noise, and were "eager for the fray." They started as if the fire was after them in the direction of the noise, and were so light and quick in their movements that they scarcely produced any sound as they pursued the game swiftly through the jungle, which was in a part of the forest where the underbrush was not very thick. The tall trees above our heads were splendid.

By-and-by we heard the dogs bark, and then the sounds of fighting with the monkeys, and their screams of pain as the dogs bit them; so we rush as fast as we can toward the scene of action. Ipay and Agounga had got hold of a big nkago, as big as one of themselves. Its mouth was armed with four large, sharp-pointed, and dangerous-looking *canines*, which had already inflicted some fearful bites on the dogs, covering them with blood. The fight must have been desperate before we came up, to judge from the condition of the dogs, and it was far from being finished. As we made our appearance, Ipay was holding the monkey by the back of its neck, while Agounga held it firmly by the back above its tail. The monkey made a desperate effort, and with one of its strong paws seized a leg of Ipay, which it put into its mouth and gave a fearful bite. A scream of pain came from Ipay, and he let his grip go. This, instead of frightening the dog, made him more furious than ever, and, like a tiger, he seized the monkey again, but not before it had given him another awful bite on the neck, which Ipay did not seem to mind. A great struggle ensued. The nkago disengaged itself once more, and again Agounga seized it by the neck and shook it as hard as he could. The monkey was losing his breath, for he had fought so hard, and the dogs were in the same condition. I wish you could have heard the noise—the nkago's cries and moans, the dogs' snarls and growlings, and our cries of encouragement. It was an exciting scene; and the racket, as it resounded through the forest, was almost deafening. The dogs were perfectly infuriated, and acted as if bound, provided they could not kill the monkey, not to let him go till we came to their assistance. They would have rather been cut to pieces by the powerful canines of the nkago than do that.

The fight was desperate. The dogs had tasted blood, and had become ferocious. I expect that they were very glad to see us come to the rescue, especially when Okabi, with a powerful blow of a dead branch of a tree he had found, hit, with a strong arm, the head of the poor nkago, and struck him senseless. Okabi then seized the nkago by the tail, and hurled its body with tremendous force twice against a tree, thereby killing it outright. The dogs, though covered with blood and badly wounded, were frantic, and acted as if they would like, if they could, to devour the monkey. Okabi allowed them to lick the unfortunate animal's blood. Poor dogs! they were badly cut, and after the excitement was over they looked thoroughly exhausted.

This nkago proved to be a large and old female, and I at once perceived that she must have had a young one with her. Suddenly I heard a little plaintive cry, and, raising my head from a surgical operation upon which I was engaged on Ipay's leg, I saw, on the top of a little tree not far off, "a child" nkago. He looked at us with his frightened eyes, and we looked at him. He tried to go higher up the tree, but could not do so.

"Hallo, Okabi!" I shouted, "let us capture this little fellow. I am sure it is the 'child' of the one we have killed." The dogs once more became infuriated. Agounga and Ipay barked with anger, and jumped up at the tree as high as they could, evidently forgetting their wounds. Their eyes were glistening; and woe to the little fellow if he fall on the ground, for I was sure he would be strangled by the dogs before we could have time to rescue him. The more we told the dogs to keep still, the louder they barked, and the more fierce they seemed to be. At last Okabi cut the branch of a tree for a whip, and, threatening to give them a sound thrashing with it, drove them a little way off by the flourish of his menacing weapon.

The little fellow was so small that it was with great difficulty he could move from one branch to another. Being of much less weight than friend Okabi, I ascended the tree, which could, however, hardly bear even my weight, and then came the tug. The diminutive animal was perfectly frightened; fright gave him strength, and he moved quickly from branch to branch. At last I succeeded in getting hold of the end of his tail. He gave a shriek, but I was determined not to let him go, and, gradually dragging him toward me, I gave him a grip on the neck with the left hand, and held him firmly. He tried to bite, but it was of no use.

How nice the little baby monkey we had captured was! He was a dear little fellow; and, after thinking for a while, I said to Okabi, "Let us call him *Jack*." So our new friend afterward was always called "*Jack*."

For a while I looked at this queer little creature. He had a bluish-black face, and his little ears looked wonderfully in shape like the ears of a human being. His lips were small, and when he opened his miniature mouth he showed a few half-grown teeth. His long, little hands were so queer! his fingers were slender, and his nails looked wonderfully like human nails. His eyes appeared somewhat dark. His body, with the exception of his face, and the palms of his hands and feet, was covered with hair, and his fingers had short hair between the joints. He had, like his mother, a crown of brown or maroon hair on the top of his head, while the eyelids had a white hue, which gave him a singular appearance. I wondered why, after all, some monkeys looked so much like human beings.

We took him home, and, after a few hours, he seemed less frightened. I was very glad it so happened at the time that there was a goat with me that had a kid, so poor little Jack was sure to have some milk to feed upon, and I wondered if the goat would not adopt Jack also for her own. That same day I tried to make Jack suck the goat, but could not succeed, the goat making too much fuss about allowing the little nkago to have the rights of an offspring. When she saw him she would raise herself on her hind legs, and butt against the little fellow, and would have no doubt killed Jack if I had not taken care of him.

For a few days I gave little Jack milk, and he began to know me well, and to get very tame. I fetched soft little berries every morning for him, and how glad he was when he saw me coming with them! After a week he did not care to taste milk at all. Water and berries were his only food.

Jack grew bigger and bigger every day, and at last came to be a strong monkey. I know that you will like to hear a great deal about Jack, how he grew up, and what he did.

Jack and I became great friends. He would go with me in my rambles, and I can not tell you how useful he was sometimes to me. I remember once I was in the woods without food and very hungry. As I walked I saw a tree loaded with a bright kind of red fruit, and I wondered if it were good to eat. Jack was following me, and I gave him some of the berries, which he immediately devoured. Now I must tell you that monkeys are said never to make a mistake in their food, and that they never injure themselves by eating poisonous fruit. What was good for Jack was, I thought, good for me. So I tasted the berries, and, finding them to be of a pretty good flavor, I ate heartily of them, without any fear of being poisoned.

Jack used to like to be petted, and now and then would delight in a frolic with me. Sometimes you might have seen him on the top of my head busily engaged in tumbling my hair; next he would be on my back pulling my clothes; and then again he would come into my hut and run away with my shoes, and carry them outside, sometimes putting them where they could not be found excepting after a thorough search.

He was full of mischief, and would break any thing that was in his way. It was of no use to lock up bottles, plates, or cups. He must have his nose in every thing, and put his fingers into every pie. One day I heard a great crash at Washington. It was in the pantry. Jack had succeeded in getting in there, and in pulling down

JACK PLAYING TRICKS.

upon himself a pile of plates. After he had done this mischief he decamped, and did not make his appearance till the next morning, for he knew very well that he would get a flogging. There was a little grove of trees near Washington, and there he disappeared. When I went there to fetch him he dodged me, for Jack was a great dodger.

Of course you will say, "How came Jack to be in your settlement at Washington?" Jack Nkago was on his way to New York, and was waiting there for a vessel to take him. I know that you will be pleased when I tell you that Jack at last reached New York. There were no amounts of capers he did not carry on on the voyage. The galley, or kitchen, was the object of his special attention from morning to night, for he knew that there, or round it, food was to be found. He would watch for the cook to get out, and then down the ropes Jack would go, seize something, and rush up again, the cook hard after him with a broomstick. Here, when out of the cook's way, he would make faces at him, give a bite or two at what he had stolen, and then grin once more at the cook, as if he would say, "I do not care for you; you can not catch me;" and then he would make more faces, and up to the very top of the mast he would go, stay there a little while, and then jump from one rope to another. He was a great friend of the sailors, and would be by them at their meals. He had no objection to tea and coffee well sweetened, to a piece of sea-bread, or a cracker. If he was not hungry, he had on each side of his mouth a pouch (a natural bag) where he could store his food till the time when he felt like eating again.

These nkagos have big pouches, and find them very useful. Jack seemed to have an especially big one, which had an unlimited power of extension, to store his food in, for when I gave him something nice, and he was not hungry, he would store it away, and then eat it at leisure afterward. When the pouch was full it looked very queer.

When Jack Nkago reached the port of New York, that city seemed to be quite a new sight to him, and very different from the African villages he had been accustomed to; and, when at first he was taken through the street, he was very much frightened. He did not know what to make out of the horses, but soon got over his terror. At last I gave Jack to a friend of mine who had some nice girls and boys, and Jack departed for his new home in Newark, New Jersey, and there, I assure you, he had a glorious time. It was at my friend Mr. Rankin's, who had a big garden for him to play in, trees to frolic upon, and boys and girls to be his playmates.

One day he got out into the street, and then upon the trees on the sidewalk, and it was a long time before friend William could coax him to come down.

Jack Nkago, I am sorry to say, turned out to be a great thief, and I remember the last time I saw him in one of his depredatory expeditions. It was in my friend's garden, and he was just coming out of the kitchen, holding a big tomato in his mouth, and two others which he carried in each hand. This was, of course, all he could possibly steal at once, as he could not take any more, and he had to walk off on his hind legs in an almost upright position, making for some quiet place where he could eat and hide his plunder in safety; but when he heard my voice shouting to him "Jack Nkago, what are you doing?" he dropped one of the tomatoes in a fright, and ran away to hide.

Several years have passed since those events in Jack Nkago's life took place. Poor Jack is now no more. He is dead; but I shall, for a long time to come, remember him.

CHAPTER XVII.

THE WONDERFUL WHITE ANTS. — THEIR DEPREDATIONS. — THEIR CURIOUS BUILDINGS.—I DESTROY THEM.—THE SOLDIERS AND THE WORKERS. — HOW THEY TAKE CARE OF THE WOUNDED AND YOUNG.

You and I, young folks, have been traveling together for a long time in an almost impenetrable forest of Equatorial Africa. We have seen many strange things of which we never dreamed before, and we have studied the habits of man, beast, and insect. At almost every step we take in that wild country we meet with new objects to gladden our eyes and cheer us in our lonely hours; and now I am to describe to you one of the most wonderful insects with which we had become acquainted during our wandering; and what I am going to tell you is based upon days of observation, which were carefully noted in my journal. The study of the *termites*, or white ants, was most fascinating to me, and helped to spend very many pleasant hours, and I hope the description of these wonderful creatures will be as interesting to you as they were to me. The only fear I have is that I shall not be able to describe the settlements and habits of these strange insects as well as I would like to do. I not only wish to amuse you, but I wish to instruct you.

First let me tell you that there was nothing in that great country of Equatorial Africa that gave me more trouble than these white ants. They were the silent enemies of which I was always afraid. I was in constant dread of them. Not that I was afraid that they would attack me, for they are very inoffensive to man personally; but they are the greatest sneak-thieves that can be found in the world, and nothing but the most constant watching and care can keep your property out of their reach, and even with the greatest vigilance they still get the better of you sometimes, for their ways of getting at your things are so sly and so difficult of discovery that it is often impossible to find them out till it is too late. Frequently they came from under the ground, and the richest man in worldly goods may become a poor fellow before he knows it. I need not tell you that, as I had to travel with a great many goods of which these little sly robbers and destroyers were very fond, I had to be on the alert all the time, but in despite of all my watchfulness they would now and then succeed in destroying my property. Many and many a time they got the best of me; and, before I describe these wonderful little creatures to you, I must tell you how I made my first acquaintance with them. Of course, in the beginning of my arrival in Africa I was rather "a green horn." I did not know much, and I did not know how many sly and silent enemies I had to contend with; so do not be astonished at my mishaps. The first time I discovered that these white ants had destroyed my property I did not feel in a very pleasant mood, especially as my stock of goods and clothing was rather low.

One fine Sunday morning, which was, as at home, a day of rest for me, I thought I would dress up finely. I knew that I had a little pine chest where I kept some very nice shirts that were still fresh with the iron and starch of home. These were, of course, only put on for great occasions, such as the Fourth of July, my birthday, or when I wanted to impress a king with my greatness. In that latter case I would let my shirt fall over my pantaloons, for the effect, in the eyes of these wild Africans, was still more beautiful, and often I wanted to please them and not myself.

I unlocked the chest and opened it. It was empty—there was no mistake about it. It was certainly the chest, and the contents that ought to have been in it were written on the lid. Only a few days before I had opened it and put in letters from dear friends, for it happened to be handy for me at the time. There could be no mistake; but the letters had also disappeared.

A clear sweep had been made of all the contents of the chest. Not a single thing had been left in it!

Could the people have dared to rob me? No! Besides, the chest was locked.

Shirts, cotton pantaloons, cotton socks—every thing gone. I could not understand the mystery at first. I was puzzled, and am sure you would have been puzzled also. When, suddenly, looking carefully at the chest, I saw streaks in the wood at the bottom that looked queer, and which had an appearance as though the wood had been eaten up in many places; and, besides, the boards of the chest were full of little black spots. When I saw at the bottom the buttons which had been on my pantaloons and shirts, the mystery became greater. I got hold of the chest, and as I raised it I saw that it had been perforated in many places; the bottom was almost eaten up outside, and nothing but a mere shell was left of the plank which was the bottom of the chest. The mystery began to get clearer to my mind when a native entered my hut, and, as he saw me, in complete bewilderment, still looking at the chest, he shouted, "The nchellellay have eaten your things."

The nchellellay were white ants.

I tell you I did not like it at all to have all my fine things eaten by the white ants. I wished they had been all at the bottom of the sea. Good-by to my fine clothing and my good show before the kings.

They had come from their subterranean abode right under the chest, eaten the wood at the bottom, entered through the crevices they had made, and then devoured every thing. Two or three days were more than sufficient for them to commit the havoc. In fact, they are, in many districts, the pest of the country, and it is a good thing the natives have no clothing to take care of.

The incident I have just related was my first acquaintance with the termites, or white ants; but, believe me, it was not the last, and I have had my things destroyed by them many and many times since.

Now I must describe the white ants to you. There are several species of termites in the equatorial regions of Africa, each building a different kind of structure, which form most conspicuous objects in the regions I have explored. These ants are of wonderful diversity, both in the form of the body and head, and in their architectural tastes and the manner they build their shelter; but all have a common affinity in their intense dislike to light, and consequently their working at their building during the night.

All the termites are miners, and they live in vast colonies or settlements, which I will endeavor to describe to you. The "termes bellicosus" form buildings which sometimes reach the height of fifteen and twenty feet, and even higher. Just think of the amount of patience and perseverance it requires. How well built these settlements must be, for, when constructed, they last for years.

The size of the termes bellicosus is about half an inch or a little more. So, for the sake of comparison, let us for a moment calculate what sized building they would make if they were of the same proportions as man. These buildings would be more than a mile in height! Would not that be wonderful?

I have studied the habits of four species of termites, of which I am going to give you an account. These were the mushroom-hived termites, the tree termites, the bark termites, and the forest termites. The latter is a species of termes bellicosus.

Now I will commence with the mushroom-hived ants. This species forms the most picturesque building, and in some districts they are found by thousands and tens of thousands together, for the most part on the open prairies which I met during my explorations. I remember well the grandest sight I saw of the mushroom building. I had just emerged from the great forest into an open prairie, situated in a country called Otando, which is about eighty miles south of the equator, when, lo! what do I see? All over the country an immense number of objects, which appear to me, in the far distance, like gigantic mushrooms. These are scattered by thousands and thousands, and are built by what I have called the *Mushroom-hived Termes.* On the following page you may see an engraving of these buildings.

MUSHROOM-HIVED TERMES AND TREE TERMITES.

They have exactly the shape of a gigantic mushroom, the top of which is from twelve to eighteen inches in diameter, and the column about five inches; the total height is from ten to fifteen or eighteen inches.

After the grass has been burnt the country presents a most extraordinary appearance. In some places these hives are met with at almost every step. There are not two exactly of the same proportions as they appear at a distance, and, when you come close to them, their difference in roundness, or sharpness of their summits, or in the thickness of the column is manifested. Not only do they differ in shape, but some are very much larger than others, as you may see by the engraving before you.

Some of them have three roofs, connected with each other by a column, the top roof being the smallest. See! and you may judge how strange such a sight was to me.

This Otando prairie might have been taken for a big country of the termites, and the buildings might have been called the cities and the villages. Now and then a few buildings, very close together, formed a cluster which might have been called a settlement; and, indeed, I have not made my mind up that these settlements, or clusters, do not communicate with each other.

Many a time I have wished that I could understand the white ants, and wondered if they had a language of their own, for such intelligence as you will see by the description I am going to give you I never met with before among the beasts and the insects I had studied.

After a few days of wonder in that far off Otando prairie, I made up my mind not to leave the country till at least I could learn as far as possible the mysterious ways of the white ants; and now let us go to work together, and do you follow me in my work, and I am almost sure you will be interested, and perhaps you will fancy yourselves really to be with me.

You will ask yourselves, Of what are these mushroom-hived buildings made? They are built of a kind of mortar formed of the earth they eat, after it is digested in the stomachs of the ants, which, by contact with the air, becomes very hard, and able to resist for years the storms of rain and the powerful rays of the sun. The buildings erected by the different species of termes are constructed to protect them against the inclemencies of the weather, against their enemies, which are very numerous, and which include many predaceous kinds of fellow-ants, and especially against daylight; for the white ants can not bear daylight, and the rays of the hot sun kill them outright, often in less than half a minute.

Early one morning I left the strange village where I was, taking with me, besides my gun, an axe; and so the people wondered what I was going to do, though none dared to follow me, as they were all afraid of me; for, alas! the plague had been in the country, and I was accused of bringing death and desolation with me; at least some believed it, while I am happy to say that many did not believe I was an evil spirit, who delighted in killing people that had shown me nothing but kindness. I remember how sad I felt to think that any of these benighted people thought such things of me.

I came soon to a cluster of these mushroom-hived buildings, and felled, with one blow of the axe, one of the structures, and I found that the base of the pillar rested only slightly on the ground, leaving a circular hollow foundation, in the middle of which is a ball of earth full of cells, which enters the centre of the base of the pillar, and these lower cells are eagerly defended by a multitude of the soldier class of ants, which I took first to be males, all striving to bite the intruder with their pincer-like jaws. On breaking open the ball of which I have spoken to you, which, when handled, divided itself into three parts, I found them full of very young white ants in different stages of growth, and also of eggs. The young ones were of a milky-white color.

I again set to work—one, two, three blows—and break and crush the upper part of the structure.

What do I see? Cells which, for the first time since they had been built, had seen daylight. There were a great number of them, all communicating with each other. The inhabitants of these dark abodes were in great dismay. To and fro they moved as if to say, What is the matter? what has happened? who has been bold enough to demolish our structures?

These inhabitants were queer looking. A great many of them had tumbled down with the ruins and debris, and among them were many young ones and a number of eggs.

How eagerly I looked, and how strangely every thing appeared to me!

I must give you a description of the inhabitants, and the engraving below will give you an idea of their shape.

First, there were a great many full-grown individuals,

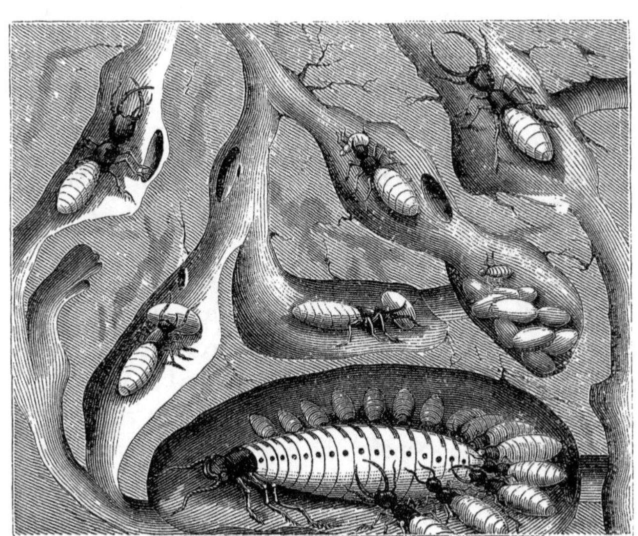

IN THE CELLS—QUEEN, SOLDIERS, AND WORKERS.

who were armed with tremendous long pincers or nippers, which could inflict very painful bites; these I took to be males, but they were soldiers. You will see afterwards why they are called soldiers.

There was another kind much shorter; they have not elongated nippers like the soldiers, but have very bulky abdomens, and appeared to all purpose inoffensive; they were of a yellowish color, with a grayish tinge, on account of the earth or mortar they had in their abdomen. These were the workers, and you will see by-and-by why they are called workers.

These two apparently distinct species had tumbled down, with a great many young ones of different sizes —some so young that they could not walk—and a good many wounded by the breaking of the building.

After looking at these for a short time, I examined the cells which I had partly demolished. These cells were elongated, and no two were exactly of the same shape. They were about one inch in length more or less, and a third of an inch broad, all the cells communicating with each other by a tunnel or corridor.

Then I saw, at the opening of each cell that had been partly broken, soldiers who came from the inside to look on and see what was the matter. They only came to the light, and then retired.

In the mean time a great scramble had taken place among the white ants that had been thrown out of the cells when I demolished the building; and I shall never forget how astonished I was when I saw them suddenly wander through the scene of the battle-field, if I may use the expression, attending to their sick and wounded. They took no notice of those that were dangerously wounded, but carried away only those that were not beyond hope. Of course the dead were left; and how careful they were to bring into the cells the wounded and young ones between their pincers! I was perfectly amazed. Human beings coming out of a railway crash, or people surrounding houses that had tumbled down, could not have developed more intelligence. I wish you could have seen how careful the workers and soldiers were in looking for the wounded after the battle, in bringing in the wounded and the young!

They even brought in those that were too young to walk. The eggs were brought in also; all were carried into the interior recess of unbroken cells, and there my sight ended. Oh, how I wished to see more!

This transportation of the wounded, young ones, and eggs was but a short work. I could hardly believe my eyes, for so many had come to the rescue from the inside, which added a great deal to the strength of those who were not wounded outside, and they all went right to work with as much system as if nothing had happened. Of course I had missed a good deal that had taken place elsewhere by watching this operation. So I demolished another shelter with my axe, and paid attention to something else. First I demolished a small part of the building, and, as soon as the cells were broken, a few head men or chiefs were seen; these were larger than the soldiers; each one moved his head all round the aperture, and then disappeared into the dark galleries, apparently without depositing any thing, for I looked on closely with a powerful magnifying-glass, and I could see nothing. But certainly there must have been a reason for coming, only I could not find out.

These very large white ants I suspected were really the males, but I could not be certain, as they had disappeared in their dark recess, where no human eye could follow them. The soldiers made their appearance, looked on, and kept still. Again, with the help of my powerful magnifying-glass, I could not see what they were doing. Then the workers came forward, and each of them turned round and ejected from behind a quantity of liquid mud or earth into the aperture. This liquid hardened as it came in contact with the air, and each little load that was discharged was put carefully on the top of the other in as business-like a way as human bricklayers would lay bricks in building or repairing a wall. Their work was managed with such precision that it would have done honor to the best bricklayer or stone-mason. I must own I was astounded. Though I had seen many ant-hills, I had never taken the trouble to know how they were made. The most strange thing was, that after an ant had deposited its load, it with great rapidity disappeared inside, following a line of retreat, and another, with as much quickness, made its appearance, so that there was no loss of time. A load was put on the top of another certainly far more quickly than a mason would put a brick on the top of another in building a wall. They continued working, till finally the breach I had made in each cell was perfectly walled up.

The question to my mind was to know if the same ants went away to eat more earth and came again. How much I would have given to see into the dark recess of the chambers! but I do not see how this will ever be done.

After a very short time, all the apertures or breaches

that I had made were closed, so they felt once more safe in their fortress from their enemies and from daylight.

I had become so intensely interested in my observations that I was covered with perspiration. I must confess I had, during my years of traveling, seen nothing more curious.

The sun was going down very fast, so I returned back to the village, promising myself to study the white ants every day for some time to come.

CHAPTER XVIII.

MORE ABOUT WHITE ANTS.—TWO SPECIES.—TERRIBLE FIGHT BETWEEN THEM.—THE WORKERS AND THE SOLDIERS.—THE QUEEN.—SHE IS SURROUNDED BY SOLDIERS.—OTHER SPECIES OF ANTS.

After my return to the village the people began to look at me with perfect amazement and with great fear; they almost appeared to regard it as something supernatural that I should demolish these white ants' buildings. "What does the Moguizi mean?" said the Otando people. "If he did not mean something, he would not have gone and staid so long looking after these nchellellays." Poor people! they could not understand why I did go, in despite of all the explanations I gave them. They could not comprehend that it was possible for a human being to care how the white ants built their shelters and what they did.

So, early the next morning I started again. I took an axe with me as before, and very soon, if you had been close by, you would have seen me hard at work demolishing one of these ant-hills. It required several blows before I succeeded, for the material was hard, and difficult to break.

While I was busily but quietly demolishing and looking on at the cells and at the havoc I had made, and the great dismay I had put the ants to, I suddenly discovered that there was another distinct species of white ant mixed up with the proper architects of the edifice.

The fighting fellows, the soldiers of this other species, were much smaller and more slender, and somewhat of a darker color, and commenced a conflict with the other "soldiers," whom I described in the last chapter, with terrific rage. I could not make out how these fellows, who could fight with such fury, could live together in the same building. On close inspection, I found that these slender fellows came out of cells with a yellow earth, while the others inhabited cells of black earth like the structure. The yellow color was due to a coating of some foreign substance on the walls of the cells. The chambers inhabited by the slender species were smaller, and did not at all communicate with those occupied by the lords of the manor, but were inserted into the vacant spaces or partition walls between the other cells. They were smugglers, and had, no doubt, introduced themselves after the buildings had been finished, from under the ground. Pretty smart fellows, I thought.

What a fight! A regular battle. No enemies could fight with more fury, with more pluck and determination. It was quite marvelous to see how the soldiers of the one kind seized the bodies of the others with their powerful pincer-jaws. The fight became general, and the larger kind showed no mercy to its less powerful enemy. Here were two fellows squaring it—a powerful big soldier against a smaller one. The fight was short. The weaker kind was killed soon. The soft body or abdomen seemed to be the vulnerable point. The soldiers of the smaller and slender kind possessed also long, pincer-like jaws, and these were powerful and formidable enemies of the workers of the larger kind, for, though much smaller in size, they had far more powerful and elongated pincers.

Suddenly a worker of the larger kind seized a small worker in its last struggle for life, when one of these slender soldiers that was passing by ran to the rescue of its kindred in species, seized the larger kind with its pincers, and, snapping them into the abdomen of the assailant, twice its size, killed it instantly. The slender one then fell from the short pincers of the larger worker who had been killed, but life was extinct. The rescuer examined the body, and, seeing that there was no life, left it on the battle-field instead of carrying it off, went away, and disappeared in search of more enemies to conquer. In the combat, every where, there was nothing but fighting, and it was no child's play, for many and many lost their lives in the conflict; it was a regular pitched battle, and I must say I was perfectly astonished at the bravery of these white ants.

By this fight I discovered that the vulnerable point of the termites is the abdomen; it is evident that their powerful pincer-jaws are made for wounding and piercing, while the structure of the workers show their short pincers are made for the purpose of labor, and that they are not great fighters. Nothing astonished me more in those deadly combats than their impetuous mode of attack. The weaker species knew the vulnerable point of his formidable enemy, who was frequently too busy fighting to know what was going on round it, and could not protect itself.

A farther examination showed me that the mushroom-like cap of the whole edifice I had demolished was com-

BATTLE OF THE WHITE ANTS.

posed of both black and yellow cells. This curious mixture of two species, each building its own cells in the same establishment, astonished me.

After this fight I went to see what had become of the buildings I had partly demolished the day before, and the operations of which had been closed at once by the white ants to keep the light out and enemies from getting in. My astonishment was great when I saw that they had, during the night, built the structures exactly as they were before I destroyed them. They continued to rebuild in the original shape, but during the daytime they only closed the cells. I noticed that now and then some of the workers brought in their pincers very large grains of sand or minute pebbles, and deposited them in the mud, and several of the cells I demolished were filled with these little pebbles.

Strange to say, the termites called workers have nothing else to do but to work and work, while the soldiers, apparently, have nothing to do. Now I must look for a queen ant. But, before doing so, I must try to tell you how their building material is formed. The earth which they eat, and which they use in building, as I have told you before, is seen through the thin skins of their bodies. This mud is mixed with a gluey matter through the power of digestion, and when it is ejected it gets hard, and with this material they construct all the buildings, tunnels, and walls which form their cells, showing a bright example, even to us all, of what time and perseverance can do. They achieve, mite by mite, the firm and solid structure of the entire hut, which stands against the storms for a good many years. Sun and rain are equally fatal to these white ants; thus it is necessary that they should build a hive impervious to light, heat, and rain. I have put white ants in the sun, and they were shortly afterward killed by its heat. I had often thought that each cell was perhaps inhabited only by one ant, but the great number I saw in each mushroom-like edifice makes it quite improbable that it should be so. Many cells are almost an inch in length, and about a third of an inch broad.

There are several species of white ants, as I have told you; some live in subterranean dwellings unseen by the eyes of man, and suddenly make their appearance through the floor of one's hut during the night, and devour all substances made of cotton or paper, for they are exceedingly fond of paper. They are very fond of eating wood, and are often found in dead trees, the wood of which they gradually devour, leaving but the outside. They must also have a great sense of smell.

One may retire to bed in fancied security, with no signs of white ants about, and in the morning wake up to find little covered ways overspreading the floor, and over the chest in which one's treasures are, and the contents of the chest partly or entirely destroyed. In a few days a store-house of goods would be spoiled. So the utmost care has to be used in keeping away the white ants. I was fortunate that my settlement of Washington was situated on a sandy soil, for in such soil the white ants can not live, on account of not being able to eat sand; and, besides, their tunnels could not be made in such a soil.

I was very anxious to find the queen—the head of the colony, the sovereign of the establishment. So I went to work, and was soon rewarded for my labor. I discovered a queen, and the engraving shown at page 123 will give you an idea of the queer shape a white ant queen is. After demolishing the building carefully, piece by piece, at last I came to a large chamber several times larger than any other, in which I found the queen. She was surrounded by the soldiers, which seemed to keep guard over her majesty, while workers were in the act of carrying away the eggs which she had recently deposited. As soon as the cell where the queen was had been partly broken, the soldiers appeared perfectly infuriated, and opened and gnashed their powerful nippers. I placed a little piece of wood as if to touch the queen with it; they threw themselves upon it, and with their nippers seized it and bit it furiously. The queen seemed almost in a torpid state; she was over an inch and a half in length, and she was continually laying eggs, the workers' business being to take these eggs to different parts of the building.

It was easy, at a single glance, to see that it had been utterly impossible for the queen to enter that chamber of the size she was.

This will bring me to explain to you how a queen is made.

Once a year a number of white ants in each colony, trained up from the eggs, come to maturity, acquire wings, and fly out of the hive or building on warm evenings. These are males and females; but very few escape, on account of the great number of their enemies, and those who do survive all dangers become the kings and queens of new hives.

The sole parents of a colony are a single female or queen, and a slender insect called the king. Possibly there may be several males, though this latter can never be seen in the confusion of the demolition of the building, and on account of the male being very similar to the soldiers.

As you have seen, the queen lives in a much larger chamber than all the rest of "her people," in the middle of the building, generally near the base of the hive, and does nothing but lay eggs, and the workers carry these to other parts of the hive.

The question naturally arises, How is the building first made? I suppose that the female intended to form a colony is seized by numerous ants, which carry her away, and from under the earth either begin a new building, or take her to a cell which had been built beforehand for the queen of a colony.

A queen is found in each colony, and, when once there, she never stirs, her chamber being devoted to her sole use.

At each end of the chamber of the queen are two holes, which communicate, like all the cells, with the other parts of the building, through which soldiers and workers can get in and out. After the queen has been installed there she loses her wings. The king, which I have never been able to recognize with certainty, loses his wings also. Then a wondrous change takes place in the queen, and from an ordinary winged ant the change, or rather transformation, becomes so great that an ordinary observer would not recognize as the queen the winged insect he had seen a few days before.

She loses her wings, though of course her head, thorax, and legs retain their normal and former dimensions; her abdomen begins to swell, and becomes so elongated and so large that it attains almost two inches in length among the mushroom-hived ants; among the large termites, to three or four inches. The head is almost lost sight of, and the creature looks more like a caterpillar than any thing else, and the exit from her house is so small then, that, even if the queen could move, she could not get out. She is imprisoned for life, and the number of thousands and thousands of eggs she lays is almost incredible. These are carried to every part of the building by the workers, while the soldiers keep watch over her. So we may say truly that the queen is the mother of her own subjects.

Besides the species of white ants I have spoken to you about, there are several others—the tree ant, the bark ant, and the forest ant.

I will speak to you of the *tree ant* first. In the forest there is a species which makes its hives or nests between the ribs of the trunks of trees. The nests are from four to seven feet long, and six to eight inches broad, and are formed externally of several slanting roofs, one above the other. The ants that make these structures have long black bodies and white heads, and are unlike the mushroom-building ants. (See page 120 for engraving.)

The structure begins from the ground in a somewhat irregular cylindrical piece of walling or building about a foot high, but varying to as much as eighteen inches, and full of cells and galleries; then occurs the first slanting roof. The larger the structure, the more of these slanting roof-like projections it possesses, and they become smaller toward the top, the middle roof being the broadest; sometimes a few inches will separate one roof from the other; the roofs communicate with each other through the cells by the same cylindrical piece of masonry; the material of which the whole is built is very thick, hard, and impermeable to rain. The structure of this ant is not common in the forest; but I found several, and I could study the habits of their inhabitants.

Bark Ant.—Another much smaller species of white ant is found under pieces of loose dry bark on the forest trees, on which they feed. The colonies were composed of a very scanty number of individuals, and the ants were so small and obscure that it was not easy to detect them. They always choose trees that are old, and have these scales of loose bark on their trunks from place to place. It is under these small patches or scales that the ants live. They feed on the wood, and build covered ways, or rather tunnels, which start from the ground, and communicate to the different places where the colony has scattered itself. Now and then, scraping under the bark, I found that the settlement had moved somewhere else as soon as they had come to the green of the tree. The material which this ant uses to build its tunnels is not earth, but wood-dust. This proves clearly that these white ants, with, perhaps, the exception of one species, build their nests of the same material as they eat, but not till after it has passed through their stomachs, and received an admixture of glutinous fluid. The quantity thrown by this little species was so minute that I could hardly have seen it with the naked eye. They worked exactly like the others I have just described. I was unable to recognize the three distinct classes of individuals. There seemed to be only two sets—soldiers and workers. They worked very slowly when joining the broken portions of the tunnels I had demolished. This was accounted for by the extreme smallness of the particles of material ejected by them, and also by the fact that, in consequence of the tunnel being very narrow, only one or two ants could work at the same time.

Forest Termes.—Now I come to the largest, another species of white ant, much larger than those I have described before, and building far larger structures.

The shelters of this ant are found in the forest, and are rather uncommon; they are always found single; their light yellow color makes them quite conspicuous in the midst of the dark foliage by which they are surrounded; this yellow color comes from the soil which the ants use in building, and which they get from below the black loam.

BUILDING OF FOREST ANTS.

The height of the structure I examined was four feet and a half, and the diameter, at the broadest part, two feet and a half; after breaking one sinuosity, I found the cells to be about one inch and a half in length, and about half an inch in height, each cell corresponding with the others by corridors or round tunnels varying from half an inch to one inch in length, and about a quarter of an inch in diameter.

In demolishing the sides, I found that the thickness of the wall was only one inch before the cells were found; but I found the earth at the top much harder than on the sides, as though the builders had put a much larger quantity of glutinous matter in this part of the structure.

After breaking away three inches of this yellow top of the nest, I suddenly came to another layer half an inch thick, full of little holes or cells, so small that they had no doubt been built on purpose for the ants to remain there alone, but for what reason they required to remain alone I was unable to discover; at that time there were no ants there.

Then with the axe I gave a powerful blow, and demolished another part of the structure, which disturbed the ants from their dark chambers. I saw there the three different classes of ants: the head men, very large, with whitish body and black head (these were but few in number); the workers, with short and thick body and broad head, but not so large as the chiefs; and, thirdly, the soldiers, not so large as the workers, more slender, and possessing longer nippers. These three distinct classes were the inhabitants of this curious structure.

As I was looking at these ants, my attention was suddenly called to watch their movements. The soldiers came, and, ranging themselves round the broken cells, took their stand and remained immovable. Then the workers came; each carried between its pincers a small particle of yellow clay, which some of them collected from the broken pieces, and which stood in my sight, while others came with their loads from the cells; there were sometimes two or three busy together at the same time and in the same cells. Each ant came and put down its particle of wet clay with the utmost precision, and then with its head moved it right and left, and by so doing succeeded in making the bits stick together, and so finished the wall. Each bit was put by the side of the one left by the previous worker, who had gone to fetch more, for here I saw the same ant go and fetch fresh pieces of the same clay, which came from the structure I had broken. I observed that they never went outside the cells to get their materials. No masons could have worked more systematically.

But how could the clay which I saw them take dry become suddenly wet? I took a small reed and advanced it quietly toward some; they made a spring at it (for these ants' bites are far worse than the others) and seized it with their nippers, and then threw upon it a little whitish, thickish matter, the same stuff that made the clay wet and ready for building purposes. During the working time not one of the largest class was in sight. The soldiers kept watch, and it was only just before the wall was closed that they retired.

I give you, on the following page, a picture of the buildings of the termes bellicosus, which often reaches the height of twenty feet or more, so that you may see the great variety there is in the shape of the buildings made

BUILDING OF THE TERMES BELLICOSUS.

by the white ants in Africa, according to the different species. It will show you that there is as much diversity in the houses of the ants as there is among those of different races of men. The difference is no greater between a negro hut and a beautiful stone house, than between the shelter of the white ant living under the bark of trees, and the large structures of the more ingenious architects.

CHAPTER XIX.

LEAVE THE APINGI COUNTRY.—GO INTO THE INTERIOR.—I AM LOST.—I RAISE THE AMERICAN FLAG ON A BIG TREE.—LEAVE IT FLYING.—STARVATION AND SUFFERING.—RETURN TO REMANDJI.

Time was passing away, and I feel that I must make further exploration of the country. It seems to me, though I did not know why I had this feeling, that the Apingi did not wish me to go into another country. They were jealous, and I was afraid they did not want any other tribe to possess me. I did not tell the people that I thought so, and kept them good friends with me. That same evening, the old men were smoking their pipes under the veranda of Remandji. Old Remandji was there, and I was ready for another long talk from him about the country.

He had spoken to me, as I have told you before, of Sapadi, but this evening he talked to me of a people of whom I had never seen or heard—of men and women who were all small. There were no tall people among them. They lived in the woods, like the gorilla and chimpanzee, and moved from place to place without fixed habitations. "What!" said I, "Remandji, have you seen such a people?" "No," said he, "but slaves of mine who came from far away (pointing in the direction of the rising sun) have told me often that they have seen them." I changed at once the conversation, fully persuaded that such people did not exist. I learned that there were many tribes living in the distant mountains, and no one among the Apingi, or among their slaves, could tell where the immense forest in which you have been traveling with me, in the three volumes I have written for you, came to an end. Strange names of tribes of wild men, living in this the most gigantic jungle of the world, were given me, many of which I had never heard before. Cannibals were not known among them, with the exception of a tribe living far off in the northeast, called Moshobo. There were tribes called Madouma, Meouandji, Ngalois, Ishogo, Ashango, and others.

So I said, "Remandji, you must give me some people, for I want to wander in the forest, far beyond the Apingi country. I want to see if I can find something new, if I can see the strange men, and discover new birds and new animals." I had a vague idea that perhaps I might meet with the unicorn; at any rate, I thought I could not help seeing new things.

But I was in trouble, for I was getting very poor, and would cut a poor figure as a king. Of course I had not a dollar, for money is perfectly useless there. The people would rather have one big bead than a twenty-dollar gold piece. I mean that my stock of goods for presents to the natives was very short. I had no more red caps, and I had but very few beads left. In fact, I had only some looking-glasses, a very few yards of calico prints, a few fine steel files, knives and forks, matches, and a few other trinkets.

My clothes were entirely worn out. I had but little powder left, only five or six scores of large bullets, and not very many pounds of small shot. My medicines were almost gone. I had but little quinine, and what should I do without it if I had a return of those violent attacks of fever which from time to time get hold of me?

You would have laughed if you had seen my wardrobe. It was composed of a coat, a single shirt, and two very old pairs of pantaloons! Happily, one of them was made of very strong material, but both were full of holes, and had been mended over and over again. One pair was minus half a leg! The shirt I wore was the only one I had to my back, for I had given the other to Remandji. I had also a linen coat. It is true, it was almost good for nothing, but, nevertheless, it was very useful, for I could wear it while my shirt was drying in the sun after being washed. Besides, I had two old pairs of socks—I should rather say, remains of socks, for I do not know how to darn stockings, and consequently the holes in the heels were getting bigger and bigger every day. As for the two old pairs of shoes I had on hand, I had mended them over and over, the needle I used being that with which I sewed the skins of the wild animals I prepared.

How sorry I felt not to be richer, for I could have gone a long way into the interior. Oh how I loved to roam and wander in the great forest! How strange every thing looked to me! It was like the discovery of a new world. So I said to myself, go a little further again, Friend Paul! Never mind the shoes, never mind the quinine, never mind any thing. Go ahead for a little while more.

So one fine morning Remandji and I, with a few Apingi, left the village and once more entered the forest. We traveled entirely by compass, avoiding the eminences as far as we could. The way was somewhat rocky, and the forest dense. Roads there were none, and for the greater part of the time the rocky beds of rivulets formed our paths. Of course, these were terrible for the shoes. The very first day the heels of one pair gave out; but, fortunately, I had another pair.

Good Remandji could not stand this kind of knocking round in the woods, and telling me at last that he was too old for such work, he gave me his son Okabi for a companion, and returned home.

Our way in the woods was so crooked at times that it seemed to me as if I was really going all round the compass, and began to suspect that the Apingi either did not want me to leave their country, or did not know the roads. Several days were thus spent in wandering in the forest. When night came we would build a camp wherever we happened to be. One evening a tornado blew over the land, and broke down the trees and their branches all round us, but, fortunately, none fell on our camp, or I might not be living to write you this story of my weary wandering. I always had to sleep with one eye open, for leopards were plentiful, and their howls filled the forest during the night. The gloom of the woods was something quite appalling to the spirits. There were places where the forest was so sombre and silent that it seemed a fit place for the haunt of some sylvan monster, delighting in silence and in the shades of night. I wondered not that the natives should be superstitious, and say that such monsters do exist. They often imagine that they see them, but as they approach near to them they suddenly disappear.

The 31st of December found me in the great forest.

That evening I thanked the Great Spirit and Maker of the universe for his great kindness to me during the year that had just gone by.

The next day was New-year's, 1859. How time had fled. I had attained my manhood in that great forest searching after the mysteries of Nature. What wonders I had seen since I left home! What perils I had gone through, what warlike tribes I had met! Dangers seen and unseen I had escaped, and the end had not yet come, for I was far away from that sea which bathed the shores from which I was to get a vessel, and I knew not if I should ever reach those shores.

Oh dear! At last I could go no farther. My last pair of shoes gave out completely that New-year's-day! They were torn, both uppers and soles, and at every step my bleeding feet were more and more lacerated, till at last the agony became too great, and the strong will which had sustained me gave way. I had to stop from time to time, for I could hardly put a step foward without an accompanying scream. The pain obliged me to lie down near a brook, where I had stopped to bathe my wounded feet, but I tried hard to show I did not suffer. To add to the misery, I found that we were lost in the forest! What was to be done? Not a village could be seen. We built our camp. I mended my shoes all that evening, as well as I could, for the morrow's journey. We ate the last of our plantains. I took a mouthful of a little brandy I had, which was very precious to me as a medicine, and we went to sleep.

Thus ended New-year's-day. How different from New-year's-day at home! But never mind, said I to myself, I have seen many things which nobody else has seen.

PAUL MENDING SHOES.

The next morning my feet were so swollen that I could not force them into my shoes. We decided to retrace our steps.

On a high hill not far from our camp stood a large and very tall tree. After a breakfast of berries and wild nuts, I took from a little sack, in which it had been laid away, a little American flag; we tied it on that tall tree on the high hill. When it floated out in the breeze we all gave three cheers for the Star-spangled banner. The sight seemed to give me new courage, and I fired a salute of three guns.

As my socks were totally unfit to wear, I tore the sleeves of my shirt, and bandaged my feet carefully with them, forced them gently into my old torn, worn-out shoes, and then, giving a last look at the flag, and shouting good-by to it, I left it to float by itself in the midst of the mountains and forests of Equatorial Africa.

I suffered dreadfully on my way back. I remember that my feet got worse instead of better. When my wretched shoes were beyond even tying together with vines, I cast them away, and bandaged my feet with what remained of my shirt, but it was of little use. The stony path and thorny jungle laughed at such protection. Starvation, real starvation, with nothing to eat, was also our lot. But one day our ears were gladdened by the roar of a gorilla. We killed it, and this furnished us with food for the remainder of our journey.

At last, after many days of weary wandering, villages were seen, and finally we got into comfortable quarters at Remandji. How well I was received! These Apingi had learned to love me, and were glad to welcome me back. Old Remandji himself was overjoyed to see his Spirit, and, in order to celebrate my arrival, got jolly drunk upon palm wine.

CHAPTER XX.

I MUST LEAVE MY KINGDOM.—ASSEMBLING OF THE PEOPLE. —THEY COME TO SAY GOOD-BY.—I MAKE A SPEECH.—REMANDJI'S REPLY.—A HEAVY PRESENT.—PRESENTS TO REMANDJI.—THEY ARE SORRY I MUST GO AWAY.

At last the day is approaching when I must quit my kingdom and bid good-by to the Apingi people. I am getting very poor. When I look at the stock of beads I have on hand, I feel that it is time for me to leave, for the Apingi people think I have power to make them; and if I had none to give them they would think that I did not love them any more, and the consequence might be that they would become afraid of me. Besides, I feel very weary and lonely. Hardship and disease have prostrated my body; when I look in the looking-glass I can see how sunken are my eyes, and how hollow and pallid are my cheeks. My lips have lost their color, and my poor emaciated body says to me "what a hard time you have had," and warns me that perhaps I shall never go home. I have a longing to see the deep blue ocean again, to see my dear little village of Washington, to see the River Commi, the big pelicans that swim on it, and to get a peep at the big cranes that waddle on its shores, and the herds of huge hippopotami which are always in sight of my settlement.

A fine morning, just a little after sunrise, when the

birds were singing, I went to the hut of Remandji and told him that I wanted him to send messengers to all the villages of the Apingi, for the Moguizi wanted to leave the country, and bid the people good-by. Good old Remandji looked me in the face steadily, and said, with a sad voice, "Moguizi, must you go—must you leave our land?" Then he called Minsho, the great-grand-nephew of the King of the Ashira, who had brought me from that country of his, and said to him, "The Spirit must go back; we are all sorry, but it is his will, and we must submit."

Then Remandji, with a heart too full to speak any more, got up and disappeared back of his house, and went into the house of the Alumbi, where the heads of some of his great ancestors were, and the ochre upon which they had rested. He rubbed his forehead, the middle of his chest, and all along his arm with it, and then came out.

There was a great commotion in the place when they heard I was going.

Messengers were sent to all the villages of the Apingi country, and the next day the people began to pour in from every quarter, loaded with provisions. The village could not hold all the people, so olakos, or "encampments" were made in the forest by them. Chief after chief made his appearance. These were the representatives of all the Apingi clans. The forest surrounding our village was filled with people who had come from the mountains, from down the river, and from the valleys.

The day for saying good-by had arrived. Two seats were placed in the middle of the street, close together—

one for Remandji, the other for me. The drummers ranged themselves in a semicircle on one side, covered with fetiches. The chiefs or heads of clans had collected at Remandji's house. Suddenly the drums began to beat, and Remandji and the chiefs advanced toward my hut. The people, who completely filled the village, chanted a plaintive hymn, and when they came in front of my hut they stopped, and I came out and followed them. Remandji and I seated ourselves on the seats that had been reserved for us, while the old men and chiefs seated themselves on the ground in front of us. A profound silence reigned. Not a whisper could be heard. The eyes of every one were turned toward me.

The Ashiras who had taken me to the Apingi country were seated near me, in front, between the Apingi chiefs and Remandji and myself.

I got up, and took from off my shoulder the kendo with which I had been invested when made a king, and which I have described to you in "Lost in the Jungle," and rang it; then, with as loud a voice as I could possibly muster, I said to them, "Apingi, the Spirit, who loves you, is going away. The sun will not rise twice again over your village before I shall be far away, for to-morrow morning I shall start in the direction where the sun disappears beyond yonder forest, and where it sets. My voice you will hear no more. With your women and with yourselves I shall talk no more. Your children will not play with me any more. The ticking of my clock (pointing in the direction where it was) will go with me. Apingi, I love you. Apingi, you have been good to the Spirit. The Spirit will never forget you. Remandji, you are my friend; Remandji," said I once more, taking his two hands in mine, "you are my friend," and I looked steadily in his face.

THE SPIRIT TAKING LEAVE.

Then, ringing the kendo once more, I shouted with all my power, "Apingi, it is the last time I shall ring the kendo in your land. When you made me king you gave it to me, and as your chief I had to wear it. To you, Remandji, I now return it." But as I was ready to hand the kendo to Remandji, the people, with one voice, shouted, "Keep it! keep it in remembrance of us. Keep it, Spirit! keep it; for we want you to ring the kendo in the land of the spirits." So, in the midst of tremendous and exciting cheers, I replaced the kendo on my shoulder, and then seated myself. I have since presented the kendo to my much-venerated friend, Sir Roderick Murchison.

Then Remandji got up and said: "Apingi people, the Spirit is going away. The Spirit is to leave us. But the Spirit can not be angry with us. The Spirit has said, and you have heard him say it, that he loved me and that he loved you. To-morrow morning the Spirit is going away.. I have seen the Spirit; you have seen the Spirit. We have heard him talk, and he has given us his hands many a time. Many of the things he has given us we wear. But many have not seen him; many have been afraid of him. By-and-by, when they come into our villages and do not see the Spirit, and we tell them once he was amongst us, they will say it is a lie—it is a lie; the Spirit has never come among you."

Then he seated himself, and immediately after the drums began to beat, and the people sung:

"The good Spirit is going away.
The good Spirit is going where the sun goes.
The good Spirit will talk to us no more.
The good Spirit will not hunt any more in our woods.
The good Spirit is the friend of Remandji.
The good Spirit loves Remandji.
Oh! oh! oh! oh! oh! oh!"

Then a large anvil of iron was brought before me by two slaves, and presented to me. It was used by the people in their blacksmithing operations, and must have weighed, I thought, about one hundred pounds. It was too heavy to carry away, and, besides, as it came from a far interior country, and was not made by the Apingi, I thought the people wanted it a good deal more than I did. So I said, "Apingi, take this anvil; you want it to work upon. It would be hard for you to get another. The Spirit wants you to work, for he loves people to be blacksmiths."

Then Remandji gave me two beautiful caps made of palm leaves, done in fine crochet work. These I have always kept, and they have excited the admiration of many ladies for the neatness of the work.

Then a great quantity of food was laid at my feet—bananas, sugar-cane, pea-nuts, pine-apples, plantains, fowls, smoked fish, etc. These things made a big pile before me, and the people shouted, "Moguizi, these you will eat on your way toward where the sun sets, while you are traveling in the big forest."

Then, in the presence of all the people, I gave to Remandji my knife and fork—the very knife and fork with which the people had seen me eat every day while I was among them.

Then, taking a pair of scissors from a bag at my side, I cut off a long lock of my black hair, and presented it to Remandji, telling him to keep it in remembrance of me. Here the excitement of the people became intense. Loud shouts rang from one end of the village to the other; the people became wild, jumped to and fro, and danced and sang—

> "The Spirit has given his hair to Remandji,
> The Spirit truly loves Remandji,
> Remandji will always keep the hair of the Spirit."

When this was finished they came toward me in a half-sitting posture, looking me in the face, and clapping their hands, and singing—

> "Spirit, why do you leave us?
> Spirit, why are you going away?"

When these ceremonies were over the people separated, and returned to their huts, or to their olakos in the forest.

In the afternoon I went into Remandji's house, and, at his own special request, I covered the walls with New York papers, which I had received while in the Ashira country. They had been left for me by some stray vessel on the coast, had found their way to Washington, and from Washington had gone to Goumbi, and from Goumbi Quengueza had sent them to me at the head-waters of the Ovenga. Among them were copies of "Harper's Weekly," and of all the dailies that were at that time published in New York. What a treat it was!

He was very proud of these decorations, and said that when another Spirit came to see him he would show them to him; and if the people should say, "It is a lie, the Spirit has never come to your country," he would point to these papers as proof of his assertion. I warned him to guard against the white ants, as they are very fond of paper.

AN APINGI VILLAGE

CHAPTER XXI.

GOOD-BY TO REMANDJI.—I CROSS THE RIVER.—THE ASHIRAS FEAR THE BAKALAIS.—A BAKALAI VILLAGE.—CROSSING THE LOUVENDJI. — I MEET QUENGUEZA. — ARRIVAL AT WASHINGTON.

THE day of departure has at last come. All our provisions have been gathered. For three days past the Apingi have been coming to say good-by to me. We are on the banks of the river, and the canoes that are to ferry us over are waiting.

I am well again. My feet had been getting better every day. With the skin of an antelope I had made some kind of boots to protect them. You would have laughed if you had seen my attempt at shoemaking.

Remandji is by my side, and leads me to the river bank. I am followed by my Ashiras. We get into the canoes. Remandji and I look at each other for the last time. I take hold of his hand, blow upon it, and I am off! Soon after I stand on the bluff on the opposite shore. A wild hurra from the Apingi I have just left greets our ears. Remandji waves his hands to me. I wave mine to him, and, just before disappearing in the great forest, I fire a gun, and look back for the last time at the good old chief and at his people. As we entered the great jungle, the sound of a multitude of voices dimly reaches our ears. It is the last good-by from the good Apingi people to me.

Once more I plunge into the great forest toward where the sun sets, and shall not stop till the broad Atlantic stops my footsteps.

My first adventure during the day was to start a flock of white-nosed monkeys. I was lucky enough to kill the very biggest of the flock. But how he dogged me! He seemed to know that I was after him.

The rain had been heavy of late, and the forest was in many places muddy. Toward evening I spied a village situated in a little prairie just in the edge of the woods. I discovered it by the smoke curling up from the huts, the huts themselves being low, and overshadowed by the background and tall trees of the forests. As there was a prospect of a tornado, I insisted on going to the village for the night.

"But," said Minsho, "suppose they are enemies? Suppose some Ashira are there, and they catch us, what then?"

Pointing to my revolvers, I said, "Minsho, no one will capture you when I am with you." This seemed to reassure him.

We entered the village, the people fleeing at the same time. The old chief and a few other men alone remained. They were Bakalais. These Bakalais people seem to be scattered all over the country, for I meet them every where, and they always seem to be dreaded by the other tribes.

The chief gave me a gazelle, and called his people back. I gave them a few beads. I could not give them much, for you know I was very poor.

The chief gave me the nicest hut in his village to sleep in; but, toward midnight, I was suddenly started from my sleep by the roof of my establishment being swept off by a tornado, which had come down with fearful power. I tell you I cleared out in the wink of an eye into the middle of the street. The whole of the village was upset. There was not a roof standing. I was blinded by the lightning, and the rain began to fall by the bucketful. The thunder was deafening, and we all stood in the middle of the street, the rain pouring down upon us without mercy, and my clothes sticking to me as if I had been ducked in a stream.

The next morning we started, and had an awful time of it, for it rained hard the greater part of the day; and when at last I reached the Louvendji River, it was so swollen, and the water rushed down with such a fearful velocity, that it was utterly impossible to cross. We must build our camp close to its banks, and there wait as patiently as we could for the waters to subside.

This part of the forest seemed to be filled with bees. They came about us in great swarms, and plagued us out of our lives; and, as if this was not enough, we had also the boco, the nchouna, and the ibolai. These are old enemies of ours, as you well know. We were also tormented by several varieties of musquitoes. Our ripe plantains seemed to attract the bees. It made me wish to see all the bee-hives in the country out of the way, and I did not bless the boco, nchouna, and ibolai. The next morning I thought I should go mad with the igooguais. I have described to you all these pleasant flies in my former volumes.

In the afternoon of the following day we thought we could venture to cross, although the current was still very strong. Each of us had armed himself with a strong stick six feet long, to be used for support against the strong current, as no one could have crossed without them.

Minsho started first, and, before we knew it, he tumbled down, and rolled over in the foaming billows of the Louvendji several times, but, after a hard struggle, he succeeded in getting on his legs again, and scrambled out of the river. As the waters were subsiding fast, we waited about three hours longer, and then made another trial.

This time Minsho had no idea of putting himself forward as our pioneer. He had had enough in the first attempt. Each one advised his neighbor to go first. One of the Ashiras started, and succeeded in reaching the left bank with very little trouble; but I saw that the water was still deep, and, as he was tall and I was short, I was almost sure the water would reach above my head.

At last my turn came. I entered the water, holding firmly to my stick. The current dashed against me at a furious rate, but I held my own, and, as I approached the left bank, a long liane (vine) was held out to me. I seized it, and made a great effort to reach the bank. The water lifted me off my feet, but I held firmly, and was pulled ashore.

We continued our route, and came once more to the dreaded passage of the Ovigui. I wish the Ovigui had been in some other country. The stream was very full, and the current was running at an awful speed. It was almost up to our neck as we crossed the bridge, clinging firmly to the guards, and swept against us impetuously. We had hardly crossed when the rain began to fall in torrents. No fire could be lighted, though the night was pitch-dark, and it was no joke to receive the rain all night on our unprotected bodies. I seated myself on the little chest which once contained my clothes, and fired my gun from time to time to frighten the leopards and other wild beasts, none of us wanting to be carried off by them.

The day dawned at last, and we reached Olendo in the midst of most tremendous cheers. None of us had perished. Then I became very home-sick. I had nothing more to keep me in Africa. I was out of every thing, and I longed to leave the Ashira country. So I made preparations to start off for the sea-shore as soon as possible.

The parting day came. Every thing was ready. Olendo said good-by. The Ashira and Quengueza's people, who had come to meet me, followed me till I disappeared from the plain, and had plunged out of sight once more into the great forest.

We had hardly been gone more than two hours when, before we knew it, we were in the midst of a large army of bashikouays. Goodness gracious! I shouted, jumping as high as I could, and making a face, which showed at once that I felt the bites of these dreadful insects. They seemed to bite me every where, and they were different from the other bashikouay; in fact, these were a new species. They were larger, stronger, and much slower in their movement. Their bite was more severe. Their heads were armed with heavy pincers, which took off the flesh at every bite. We jumped high up in the air to avoid them. The men, at every bite, would say *brew, brew, brew*, which is an exclamation meaning "it hurts." It is very expressive.

At length we reached the banks of the Ofoubou. Quengueza's canoes were waiting for us. I slept at good Obindji's. The next day we started, and finally reached the village of Goumbi. Quengueza was on the shores to welcome me. How happy he was to see me. How happy I was to see that he was quite well. It did my heart good to see the best friend I had in Africa. We hugged each other in the good old African fashion among equals. I told him I had been made a king. I can stay but a few days with him. I must go. I am dreadfully home-sick.

A few days after this I arrived in Washington. Ranpano welcomed me. My houses were in good order, and nothing had been stolen from me. The people are honest, and they love me.

I must see the ocean. How it made my heart leap for joy when I saw the deep blue water! It was grand. I kneeled down on the sand, and thanked God for his great kindness to me, the poor and lonely traveler of the jungle of Equatorial Africa.

How glad I was when I returned to that dear little bamboo house of mine, and looked at the dear little akoko (my bed), and saw my little clock still on the mantel-piece waiting for me, though its ticking had ceased. How refreshing it was to see the little comforts that were to surround me once more.

I immediately went to look into several tin Japanese boxes which were full of provisions and other good things to eat. In one there was a little coffee and tea, in another some preserved meat, in others rice, crackers, etc. Not a thing had been touched. It would never have entered the head of good Ranpano or any of his people to rob me.

MY SETTLEMENT AT WASHINGTON.

I wish you could have seen how glad the Commi were to see me; how many fowls and bunches of plantains they brought me.

I was at home again; once more I was in my African home, in my little settlement of Washington. There stood piles upon piles of boxes filled with trophies of my hunting, all well preserved and well kept by the aid of arsenic, of which, when I left New York, I had taken with me one hundred pounds.

I wish you had been with me when I unpacked the big boxes which contained the immense collections in natural history I had made. You would have seen that I had not been idle. I am sure you would have been delighted with the sight of those boxes. There would come out of one a huge gorilla, a chimpanzee, or nshiego mbouvé; from another a wild boar, an antelope, or a gazelle; then from another would come out hundreds of birds, with smaller quadrupeds. Then came another box; then would come crocodiles, queer-looking turtles, stuffed fish and snakes. The next would be a box of shells, then one of insects and butterflies, and another containing otters, hyenas, leopards, squirrels, wild cats, rats, mice, and I do not know what else.

What are these big things? They are manatees. Then come three huge hippopotami. I opened their stomachs, and there came out from their inside gorillas and their skeletons, and any amount of stuffed wild beasts. Every animal I killed I stuffed and brought home, with the exception of the elephants, for I did not know how I could ever carry a stuffed elephant through the jungle. I am sure you will agree with me, it would be a most difficult work. The hippopotami, which, of course,

I killed by the river side, I could put in canoes and send to Washington by water. I have given one of their skins to my distinguished friend Bierstadt, whose magnificent paintings some of you have seen. I can assure you it was an immense work for me to carry these collections through the jungle and take them to my different dépôts, till I took them to my settlement of Washington. It would have made your heart glad to see the many species of birds and animals which were entirely new, and which I have since described before scientific societies. There were also boxes which did not contain skins of wild beasts or other specimens. You would have seen that they contained queer guitars covered with snake skin or elephants' ears. You would have seen handja, terrible-looking spears, huge square knives, long, double-edged, sharp-pointed knives, bags of poisoned arrows, sharp-pointed axes, war-axes, shields made with the skin of the elephant, and other fearful implements of war made by those savages; and you would have shouted with one voice, "Oh, Friend Paul, we wish we had been with you in those great forests of Equatorial Africa!"

And now let us take a cruise along the western coast of Africa, live a great part of the time on board of a ship, and see new countries, unlike the regions where we have been wandering together so long.

CHAPTER XXII.

THE ISLAND OF MADEIRA.—SAILING FOR SENEGAL.—A HUGE SHOAL OF PORPOISES.—THEY SWIM SO FAST.—HARPOONING PORPOISES.—REJOICING ON BOARD.—HOW PORPOISE MEAT TASTES.

Some years ago I visited the beautiful island of Madeira, where we had come to revictual after a most severe storm, under the violence of which our ship almost foundered. Our boats had been carried away, the live-stock had been washed off by the waves, our provisions had been partly destroyed, and for a few hours we were in danger of going to the bottom of the ocean. It was the first great storm I had experienced at sea, and the waves appeared frightful to me, for I was no sailor at all.

How beautiful was that island of Madeira, with its hills covered with grape-vines, and trees bearing all kinds of fruits. Bananas, pears, apples, chestnuts, walnuts, oranges, lemons, and grapes were to be found in great abundance. In fact, almost, if not all the fruits belonging to the temperate zone seem to be there, with others belonging to tropical climates.

Our vessel was called *The Roland*, commanded by a rough but good-hearted captain. I made great friends with a sailor by the name of John, who was always ready, when off duty, to do any thing for me.

For several days after leaving the island, when ready to continue our voyage, the breeze was fair and the sky clear. Only a few white, fleecy clouds were tossed about by the wind. The sun shone upon the sails of our ship all day, and made them appear of a snowy whiteness. The beautiful blue sky seemed to give its color to the sea, which appeared more blue by the contrast of the white caps of its gentle waves. How I enjoyed the breeze as it blew upon my face! I could feel that it made me strong. What an appetite it gave me. In the evening I would watch the wake of the ship, which was like a line of fire.

The *Roland* was a good sailer, and many a time we were going at the rate of ten miles an hour. We were bound for West Africa. The Senegal country was the first land we intended to put our feet upon after leaving the vessel. A few days brought us to the leeward of the island of Teneriffe. I shall never forget the time when I got a sight of the high-towering and snowy peak. It was in the morning. Not a cloud hung over the land. The island, for about a third of its height, was covered with snow. It rose before us like an enchanted land—a land which seemed to rise so high that it looked as if it wanted to kiss the sky. It rose right from the sea to a height of more than 12,000 feet.

It was a sight never to be forgotten. To this day I have this island before me. I remember well that when the shades of evening cast their gloom over the sea, this tall, giant-like island appeared to me like a ghost gradually fading away from my sight. My eyes were riveted upon the spot, though I could see nothing, till the captain called to me, "What are you doing there? You seem as still as a statue." He was right. I was thinking, when he awoke me from my deep thoughts, of the tremendous volcanic outburst that must have taken place to raise the island from the bottom of the sea—what a powerful uprising of the fiery elements below; for Teneriffe is entirely of volcanic origin. As the island faded from sight, I knew that I should probably never see it again, and I silently said good-by to it. That very same night a gale of wind blew, which made the ship roll and pitch in a way that was not comfortable. Happily, the storm lasted only a few hours.

My heart, during the voyage, was bounding with joy, for I was going to a country which I had never seen, and of which I had read so much. Senegal was to be one point we were to visit. We were going to sail along the coast which forms the boundary of the great Sahara. The navigation was dangerous, and woe to the poor shipwrecked mariner who is cast upon that inhospitable coast.

I shall see the wild Arab, or Moor; I shall ride on the back of a camel; I shall get a glimpse at the huge baobab-tree, and probably meet with all kinds of adventures.

I feel in high spirits. The voyage has thus far been prosperous. The wind has been fair a great part of the time. The health of the crew is good, and all the damage the great storm has done to the ship has been repaired; so you will not wonder that I feel happy and hopeful.

One afternoon a dead calm overtook us. There was not a ripple on the water, which was as smooth as a mirror, but the heavy swells of the sea made the vessel roll in the most fearful manner, for the sails were of no use in steadying her. They only flapped and flapped against the mast with such force that I really thought the whole rigging, with mast, would break down. Happily, every thing on board was lashed carefully to the bulwarks or to the iron rings in the deck, which were fastened to the beams underneath.

The rays of the sun were pouring down upon us with great force.

When thus becalmed, the vessel became unmanageable, the rudder was of no use whatever, and the poor ship was literally swinging round and round in a circle.

We did not like it at all. We knew that we might be becalmed for several days, and the prospect of a fair passage to Senegambia became blue as the sea. The captain hoped, however, that after sunset a breeze would spring up. We were disappointed. After sundown it did not come. I was tired out, for it was impossible for a man to stand up. I had to hold fast to a rope in order not to be flung to the other side of the vessel head foremost.

That night it was impossible for any body to sleep, and as for eating at the table, I gave it up; but I managed to eat what I could, in a very uncomfortable manner, on deck. I can tell you that in such a time we did not care for hot coffee or soup.

Oh glad was I when the morning came. At sunrise a light breeze greeted us, and soon after we were under good headway again. I was sitting at the bow of the vessel, holding fast to a rope with one hand, and watching the vessel as she went through the water, which she seemed to cut in two. Oh, how beautiful is a fine morning at sea in that region! The tropical breeze was fanning us, and seemed to come from balmy lands to welcome me. The sky was blue, and the water seemed still bluer than the sky; and the sun, as it shone upon the sea, seemed to say, "I am the source of all life in this world." The sailors, meantime, were busy washing the deck, in which the captain took great pride, it was so white and clean. The cook was busy preparing breakfast, and every thing was alive on board the good ship *Roland*.

While sitting at the bow, as I have described, I suddenly spied ahead of us an immense number of porpoises, swimming and jumping out of the water, and seeming to be migrating to some other region in the ocean. As they were moving from east to west, they were going to cross our bows, and I shouted, "Captain, porpoises are ahead of us!" He gave a look, and answered, "That is so—that is so; let us see if we can not kill one for dinner." The porpoises were moving along like a vast army, thousands and thousands of them together. Onward they swam, stopping for nothing in their migration, every now and then springing clear out of the water. And how fast they did swim! I believe the porpoise to be one of the fastest fishes in the sea.

"Get the harpoon ready!" shouted the captain. "John, take the harpoon, go under the bowsprit, and harpoon one of these fellows if you can."

"Captain," I shouted, "let me have a harpoon too; I must try to harpoon one of these porpoises."

"If you try," said he, "you must be tied fast with a cord round your waist, for, as sure as you live, if you are not made secure with a rope, you will drop into the water, and that will be the end of you. John," said he, "fasten a rope round your waist also." It was hardly said when the captain had a rope round me, as he wanted to make sure himself that I was safe. John had made himself secure. My harpoon was a real nice one, which had done good service before in harpooning porpoises, and had also gone into the bodies of a good many sharks.

By the time we were ready we were in the midst of the porpoises. They did not seem to be frightened at all by the ship, and they swam so fast that they seemed to skim through the water. Some of them must have really gone at the rate of fifteen or twenty miles an hour. I was perfectly amazed. They must have thought our ship was a big floating rock, for many would swim round and round us, and that when we were going at the rate of nine knots (miles) an hour, and seemed to make no effort to accomplish the feat. They would pass under our bowsprit with the rapidity of an express train. Three times John had sent his harpoon at them, and three times he had missed them. I had sent mine twice, and, of course, I had missed.

"John," said I, "we must harpoon one of these fellows, for I hear they are good to eat." "I bet they are," said John; "the liver is splendid eating, cooked with onions. The meat has no taste of fish, and looks somewhat like beef." This splendid prospect of a good meal made me feel more than ever that one of these porpoises must be harpooned. I was tired of pork and salt beef, and then I had never tasted of a porpoise, and wanted to know if they were really good. Some of them did not swim so fast as others. See, one is coming! John's eyes are upon it, and his harpoon is ready. I am watching; I am ready too. Down goes John's harpoon; mine goes down at the same time. I have struck a porpoise! The captain, who by this time is by me, seizes the line

HARPOONING PORPOISES.

of the harpoon. The blood of the porpoise darkens the blue sea as we slowly draw him in over the side of the ship.

John, too, has harpooned a big fellow, and the crew comes to assist in hauling him in.

There is a desperate struggle from the porpoises. It is of no avail. They are on deck. I am wild with excitement. I shout, "I have harpooned a porpoise!" I really thought I had done a wonderful thing. This porpoise measured over six feet, and what a beautiful color!

I really do not think it belongs to the same species which we have at home, for I do not remember having seen a single specimen near the African coast similar to this. These are always met in the middle ocean. The color on the back was grayish-black, while the sides were somewhat grayer, and the abdomen was whitish. It must have weighed two or three hundred pounds.

There was great rejoicing on board, for we were to have plenty of food. The cook came with his huge knife to help the sailors, and the two poor porpoises were soon cut to pieces. They had no fat whatever. The flesh was red, and not unlike that of beef. The liver, being considered by the sailors as the best part of the fish, was given to the captain.

For dinner we had porpoise steak, and it was not bad at all. Sailors being fond of onions, the steaks were surrounded with them. I did not care, as there were no ladies on board; as for the liver, it was perfectly exquisite. We had a glass of good wine after dinner that day. The sailors had a jolly time, and ate *ad libitum* of the flesh.

In the evening they felt quite jolly, and smoked their pipes with great delight, and sang a great many songs. I felt very happy to see these good sailors enjoying themselves. These poor fellows have a hard life, and we do not know how much we are under obligations to them for fetching to us from distant climes many of the luxuries we enjoy.

CHAPTER XXIII.

APPROACHING THE SENEGAL.—SAILORS' YARNS.—DANGEROUS NAVIGATION.—SHIPWRECKS OF VESSELS.—TERRIBLE SUFFERING OF THE CREW OF THE MARGARET.—OUR FEARS.—TAKING SOUNDINGS.

We were getting every day nearer our point of destination, and approaching the great desert of Sahara.

Our evenings were spent with the captain in relating our adventures. The captain had traveled all round the world, and spoke to me of strange countries where I had never been. Oh, I wished to go where he had been—to China, Japan, India, and the East Indian Archipelago. He had seen the orang-outang in its native wilds. He had been in Brazil, the West Indies, and many islands of the Pacific. But then he had not been in the equatorial regions of Africa. He had not seen the gorilla, the chimpanzee, the nshiego mbouve, or the kooloo-kamba. Now and then I would have a talk with the sailors on the forecastle, for I love the sailors dearly. Yes, they are blunt, rough if you like, but they are natural. They always say right out what they mean, and are almost always kind-hearted. Those who are not are rare exceptions.

They would frequently tell me about their wild pranks, and what a laugh we would have over some of them! At other times they would almost start tears from my eyes by telling me some of their great trials, shipwrecks, and stories of starvation and thirst on desert islands. Especially was my heart full of sympathy for them when I heard their story of their lying in port surrounded by pestilence and death, the yellow fever, the black vomit—these terrible scourges carrying away sometimes almost every body on board, and often leaving but one or two as witnesses of the terrible plague, so that they might tell the story of their sufferings to their fellow-men. At other times they would tell of their hardships on the coast of Africa, and the terrible fever they had been subjected to in the Gulf of Guinea. It was by moonlight that we had our last talk. The evenings were cool and pleasant, and it was so nice on deck!

At last the voyage drew near its close. The captain expected soon to see land. We were not to see green fields, nor hills covered with trees, but the sandy and bleak shores of the great desert of Sahara, and feel its hot winds.

The face of the captain began to appear anxious as we approached the shore, for we were nearing the famous land of Arguin, where many and many a wreck had taken place. There the Medusa found her watery grave, and many of the brave hearts that were on board died on the raft they had made, after long days of agony from starvation and thirst.

And no wonder that the captain began to feel anxious, for the navigation became more dangerous as we approached nearer and nearer to the coast of Arguin. The natives were fierce, and the shipwrecked people were either murdered, or made to suffer the most abominable kind of slavery.

At last, one afternoon, we got sight of land north of Cape Blanco. The next day we rounded the cape, and came to the Bay of Arguin, which is most dangerous to navigators on account of its numerous banks and shoals.

I began to feel anxious too. I did not care to be made a slave. I did not care to travel as the slave of a wandering Arab or Moor in the great desert. The very thought made me shudder; and I am sure, my dear young folks, that you would have felt the same, for you know what the fate of many a shipwrecked sailor has been in that part of the world. The stories of their sufferings have been published far and wide.

The evening of the day when we reached such dangerous ground, the captain related to me stories of some of the wrecks that had taken place there. I well remember that of a friend of his, who was on board of the ill-fated "William Vaughan."

The "William Vaughan" left London on the 29th of April, 1844. On the 20th of May she rounded Cape Blanco, and entered the Bay of Arguin. Suddenly the ship found itself in shallow water; but, before she could be got round, she stuck fast in the sand. Large quantities of ballast were thrown overboard, the ship was lightened, and the next day she was afloat. In the mean time, the chief mate had been sent to take soundings ahead, for all the charts were incorrect, no doubt on account of the shifting of the sand-banks. The sea being very heavy, he was obliged to anchor his boat for the night under the island. Just as he was rounding the point again to return to the ship next morning, he saw two natives and a white man coming toward the boat.

Was it possible? It was so. The white man hailed the boat in English. He was a countryman—a poor unfortunate white man that had been wrecked. The kind-hearted mate again rounded the point, where the sea was not so heavy, to take in his countryman. But the moment he landed the two natives set upon him and beat him unmercifully with bludgeons. The poor mate had landed unarmed. Revolvers at that time were not in use, though pistols were known. They would not have caught me in such a scrape. I never leave my revolvers any where, especially when traveling in a wild and dangerous country. One of the sailors hastened back to the boat and fetched a gun, which he gave to the natives, who took it and ran away, leaving the poor white man in their hands.

How glad the poor fellow must have been when he saw his countryman! How his heart must have beat at the thought that his days of slavery were over, and how he must have thanked God for his safe delivery!

Then came his sad story. He belonged to the bark Margaret, of London, which had been wrecked the preceding year, in the same month of May. Nearly all the hands had been murdered by the savages, and those who were not had been made slaves. Four more were upon the island. When they reached the vessel, and the captain was made acquainted with the facts, he immediately took means to ransom his countrymen. The natives agreed to receive a certain amount of goods, and then release the prisoners; but after they had received the amount they asked for more; and, after this second demand was granted, they again asked for more, and finally fired at the men, and compelled them to flee for their lives and to take refuge in their boats, leaving their property behind.

The boat had gone ashore well prepared. They had a small brass gun on board, but it would seem that they did not know how to make effective use of it. It appears to have been too heavily loaded, for when it was fired it recoiled with such force that one of the gunners was killed, and, in falling overboard, by some unaccountable misfortune he upset the boat, and all the ten men were either drowned or killed. Not one of them came to tell the story of their fate. The natives got possession of the boat, righted and loaded her up with warriors, and came to attack the vessel. Only four men and the captain were left on board.

It must have been a terrible moment of suspense among these five men. They knew it was a question of life or death. Every thing was ready for a deadly fight. Hatchets, matches, sabres, guns, pistols were at hand, and every thing that was heavy and handy to throw into the boat. What a feeling of anguish there must have been in the hearts of these men! All their companions were dead, and they knew that the same fate awaited them if they were captured, for these cruel savages would show no mercy.

The boat came nearer and nearer. It was swarming with savage men; but fortunately, as it came broadside, the master, who was no doubt a good gunner, took careful aim, fired and sunk her, with all on board. Then he slipped his cable, and, with only four men for a crew, sailed off. How anxious the poor captain and crew must have felt, and how much they must have dreaded those treacherous sand-banks in the Bay of Arguin, for they knew what fate awaited them if they were wrecked. How much they must have felt the loss of their brave companions, whose kind hearts and courage led them to try to rescue their fellow-countrymen. How desolate and dreary the deck of that poor ship must have seemed. The merry songs of the sailors were heard no more as they furled and unfurled the sails.

No doubt the frenzy of the savages on shore was terrible when they saw that so many of their number had perished; they must have precipitated themselves like tigers on the poor white men ashore, and cut them to pieces.

See how rash it was for these men to fire the big gun from their boat. What good could they have done? If they had killed any of the natives on shore, the white men would have been murdered instantly; so it would have been far wiser for them to go on board without firing. It shows that, in a case like the one just related, it is very important for men to be cool and calculating, to look ahead, and to let the head control the impulses of the heart.

Some of you may perhaps remember that in "Lost in the Jungle" I gave you an account of a trial for witchcraft, where a great friend of mine was accused of sorcery and killed. How I fought in my heart! I was on the point of rushing among the crowd and shooting down the natives that held her. Oh, I remember how near I was to doing it; but suddenly reason told me not to do it. It seemed to me very hard that reason should govern the kind impulse of my heart; but I let reason have the upper hand. I suppose, if I had fired and killed the nephews, and sons, and people of my friend King

Quengueza, and fled, even if I had not been killed, the good chief would have said to me, "White man, whom I love, why have you killed my people? What have they done to you? To save one you have killed several."

So what a pity it was that the men in the boat were so rash. Of course, it was hard to be attacked for nothing, and if there had been no white man ashore they would have been right in firing at the natives for their treachery. But white men had to be saved, and prudence would have been the best policy. They might have told the story to some man-of-war on the coast, whose captain would have been able, no doubt, to ransom the men; if not, he would have been able to inflict on the natives such terrible punishment that they would not have been ready to fire again.

You will not be astonished to hear, after this, that there were men constantly on the watch. One sailor was always kept at the top of the mainmast, the time of his watch being two hours, when another would relieve him. Men were continually throwing out the lead to take soundings. It is not every sailor who knows how to throw the lead, and only three on board were skillful at it. I can assure you it is hard work—an elongated piece of lead, flat at one end, and smeared with tallow, so that when it touched the bottom they could ascertain the character of the bed of the sea where the lead was cast. If it was mud, of course mud would show on the tallow, and if it was sand, sand would show, etc., etc. This piece of lead appeared to weigh about from twelve to fifteen pounds. It was attached to a long line, which could go with the lead to a depth of about sixty fathoms. Sailors always measure by fathoms (six feet).

HEAVING THE LEAD.

The sailor who was to throw the lead stood in the rigging of the foremast, just outside of the bulwark. He held the line, which was so coiled about his right arm that it would pay out easily, about six feet from the end to which the lead was fastened. Before throwing it, he would swing it a moment with great force, and then, letting go, send the heavy lead flying ahead beyond the bow of the ship before it struck the water.

CHAPTER XXIV.

AT THE MOUTH OF THE GREAT SENEGAL RIVER.—APPEARANCE OF THE COUNTRY.—A VILLAGE.—THE HOUSES.—A SANDY COUNTRY.—HOW THE PEOPLE CARRY MILK.

WE passed through the much-dreaded region without any serious mishap. Our vessel arrived before the great Senegal River, and anchored outside of the bar. I must confess that I was very glad, for I did not relish the idea of a wreck on the inhospitable shores I have just described to you.

A few days after the arrival of the *Roland*, I was quietly settled in a quaint old negro town on the seashore opposite the island of St. Louis, the chief French settlement on the Senegal River. What a queer village it was! It had stood on the same spot for several generations, on the narrow tongue of land which separated the river from the sea, a few miles from its mouth. This land might properly be called the beginning of the Great Sahara. On the left or south of the village, as far as the mouth of the river, the eye met only a continuous stretch of white sand; on the right or north, the same aspect of country presented itself to view; but as the eye followed the shore northward, the extent of country became broader, and toward the river side stunted trees and scraggy bushes or shrubs were visible on approaching its banks; otherwise a vast sandy tract of country was all that could be seen. The country presented an appearance of utter desolation, entirely unlike the great equatorial regions where I have led you in this and the three preceding volumes. How unlike the villages of the forest was this village of the lower Senegal country. It was built on the downs or sandy hills which had been formed by the sands which were constantly accumulating there by being shifted from the Great Desert by the winds blowing from it. Some of these sand-hills were quite high.

VILLAGE ON THE LOWER SENEGAL.

The houses were round, the walls built of clay collected from the river, and generally from four to six feet in height. There were no windows to these huts, and only one door led to the interior. The sharp-pointed, somewhat sugar-loaf shaped roofs were high, and thatched with straw. Inside of these huts the people cooked and slept. There were no regular streets, the houses being scattered all about, without any order or symmetry. Inside, a bullock-hide, or a mat upon sticks about two feet from the ground, formed the bed. One or two water-jars, some cooking-pots, a few wooden vases, several immense calabashes used as dishes or for washing, and one or two low stools, constituted all the furniture to be met with in these huts. A group of huts belonging to one family were surrounded by fences as a kind of wall. This town had, I should think, several thousand inhabitants. From a distance it had a very picturesque appearance, as you may judge by the picture before you, but, after entering it, the charm disappeared.

The situation of the village was certainly very picturesque. In front there was the sea, back of it the River Senegal, and then the white sand of the desert on every other side. The people were neatly dressed, in queer-shaped garments made of cotton goods.

A few little horses, some donkeys and camels which belonged to a caravan just arrived, might often be seen wandering about. But judge of my astonishment when, sauntering through this labyrinth of houses, I came to a hut in front of which were three live lions lying flat on the ground—three young tame lions. As I approached they looked at me, as if to say, "Who is this stranger?" but there was no anger in their gaze; they were young, though quite formidable to look at. They were for sale. I wondered why they were not chained, and found, on looking more closely, that they were tied with a cord by the neck.

The people of the village were of the negro race, but of a far superior type than the Congo negro. They belonged to a tribe, if I remember well, called Jaloff, and were certainly very fine negroes. They were not heathen, but very strict Mohammedans, for in the days of old the followers of Mohammed had converted them. They were generally tall, and very black, and among them some could be seen with straight noses, thin lips, and fine features. Most of them could speak the French language as well as their own, learned through constant intercourse with the French, under whose sway they lived.

The people of the village were great fishermen, their chief business being to catch fish. They were very experienced canoemen, for the whole of that coast is defended by formidable breakers, which dash against the sandy shores of the Great Desert with irresistible force. Many and many days during the year these natives find it impossible to cross over the breakers to go a fishing, and often, after making vain efforts to go through them, have to give up the attempt, after upsetting time after time.

So I need not tell you that they are splendid swimmers and canoemen. Nevertheless, accidents take place; men are drowned now and then, either from sheer exhaustion from swimming when they upset in the breakers farthest from the shore, but more generally from the canoe striking them with great force as it turns over, or by being thrown against them by the next angry wave.

They are, like most Mohammedans, fatalists, and believe that Allah (God) has ordered beforehand every thing that is ever to happen to them. The efforts of the missionaries to convert them have been of very little avail, as far as I could see.

Of course nothing could grow in that arid region, and their food had to be raised on the islands higher up the river, or near the lagoons, swamps, and marshes on the right bank, where patches of fertile land are found. The chief food used by this people is made of a kind of millet, which they pound, and call kouskous. Cattle are very abundant in Senegal, and form the chief wealth of the people of the country.

I really enjoyed the sights in this village, especially in the morning, when the people were coming to market. St. Louis, being a large settlement, with a population of twelve or fifteen thousand people, required a good deal of food, and the people would come from villages and farms situated higher up the river, where, as I have said, vegetation could be found, and where many things would grow; but a good deal of the produce came also from the left bank of the river.

It was amusing to see them come with milk in large leather bags, or bottles made of goat or sheep skins sewed carefully together, so there was no leakage; they were made just like those mentioned in the Bible, these people having made no improvement in these utensils for thousands of years. These bottles could hold sometimes as much as five gallons and more. The women carried them on their heads.

The butter was soft, and was also brought to market in the same manner—in skins. It is frequently used by the natives to rub their bodies with.

CHAPTER XXV.

THE SENEGAL RIVER.—THE JALOFFS.—THE FEHLAHS.—THE FULAHS.—THE MANDINGOES.—HABITS OF THESE TRIBES.—THE MOORS.—DESERT WINDS.—RECEPTIONS IN JARS.—"HOW NICE IT IS!"

Now that I have given you a description of the Senegal village, I must speak to you about the country.

The Senegal River is one of the most important rivers of Africa, and the colony of that name is the largest and most thrifty on the West Coast. The country belongs to France, and the forts along the banks of the river extend to a long distance into the interior. The river takes its rise in the region of the Kong Mountains, and empties into the sea in about 16° north latitude. The head or chief trading settlement is St. Louis.

From Senegal comes a very large quantity of gum arabic, amounting to several millions of pounds every year. An immense trade in pea-nuts is also carried on. These are taken to Marseilles, where soap and oils are made from them. Gold is also brought from the interior; and hides, wax, and ivory form also important articles of trade.

The people inhabiting the great Senegal country are all warlike. Among the chief negro tribes are the Fehlahs, the Jaloffs, the Fulahs, and the Mandingoes.

The Jaloffs are an active, powerful race. They are tall, very black, and their noses are not so flat, nor their lips so thick as those of the true negro; indeed, some have straight noses.

The Fulahs are much attached to a pastoral life, and their hair is soft and not very woolly. Their chief wealth consists in the possession of cattle, which have very long horns.

The Mandingoes are Mohammedan negroes, mild, and of pleasant disposition. They manufacture a good deal of cotton cloth with an ingenious loom of their own, and occupy a large tract of country.

In fact, these negroes of the Senegambia country are, I think, far superior to those found in other parts of Africa, not only in looks, but in intelligence.

But on the right bank of the River Senegal, and in the interior, live tribes of people far more powerful than the negroes, by whom they are dreaded. These are the Moors of the desert, a martial, treacherous, and vindictive race, always at war with their neighbors.

As I have said, a very great part of the gum arabic used in the world comes from the Senegal River, and the Moors possess all the country from which it comes.

These Moors have a very wild, staring look; their treachery is notorious, and they regard the negro villages that surround them the same as game, which they plunder at will, and the people of which they lead into captivity. These people are nomadic; when the heat of the desert becomes intense, and every thing there is burned up, they move southward toward the negro country, and stay there till the rains have commenced in the beginning of July, when they go northward again. It is at that time that they commit the most depredations. They despise the negroes, who are very much afraid of them.

But the negroes themselves are often at war with each other. In fact, war seems to be the normal state of Africa wherever the traveler goes.

With the negroes and with the Moors, cattle are the wealth of the country. The Moors possess great herds of cattle, and a great many horses, camels, and donkeys. The armies of these tribes of the desert are composed entirely of cavalry, each tribe being able to raise from two to four thousand horsemen.

There are three forests in which the gum arabic is produced in great quantities; these are called, if I remember rightly, Sahel, Lebiar, and Alfatack. Besides these, there are other groves of gum arabic trees in different parts of the desert. The three first-mentioned forests are claimed by three different tribes of Moors. The language of these people is, of course, Arabic, and they are named Trazas, Aulad-el-Hagi, and Ebraguana. Each tribe has its own chief. They are nomadic, and are continually fighting with each other. Their features are dark brown, but fine; their hair is black and glossy.

The gum arabic tree has a very peculiar growth. I know you would like to have a description of it. It is an acacia, not at all beautiful, from fifteen to twenty feet high when full grown; a few specimens attain a greater height, but in general it is more like a shrub than a tree. The wood is white and hard. It is very seldom that one sees a straight tree, and the trunk is covered, almost from the ground, with crooked branches of different sizes, which makes the tree not pretty to look at. The leaves are small, and under each leaf are three crooked blackish thorns. The flowers are white and small, and the seeds are contained in pods.

The month of March is the time when the harvest of the gum arabic takes place. You must not think that the gum arabic comes all in small pieces. A good deal of it comes out of the trunk of the tree in quite large lumps. I have seen pieces twice as large as an orange, and even larger, and, after breaking them open, the centre would be filled with liquid gum arabic, which was most delicious to the taste. While in the country I ate much of it, and it was often my chief food. It is very nutritious and satisfying to the appetite. It is only the red gum arabic which is often found in such large pieces. Of course, as it grows older, the liquid gradually dries up, though it does not become brittle like the white gum, some forests of which are also found near the Senegal River. The two gums are, however, entirely distinct.

There are a good many islands in the River Senegal, some of which are very fertile, and produce millet, Indian corn, yams, sweet potatoes, plantains, and bananas. At about ninety miles from the mouth of the Senegal River is a flourishing trading station, where a great quantity of gum is brought by the Moors.

The climate of the Senegal country is any thing but pleasant, being subject to sudden changes. At certain seasons of the year the hot winds from the desert make it almost unbearable. The rainy season is short, and the climate is dry the greater part of the year.

How much I suffered there from the hot weather! I remember one day a terrible hot wind from the desert begun to blow. The atmosphere was terribly heated, and the air, which seemed to come from an oven, was prostrating to the physical system. It blew from the northeast, over the scorching sands of the Sahara—sands which had been heated for months without a drop of rain to cool them. The powerful rays of the sun had been pouring upon the white sand day after day, week after week, month after month, till the whole atmosphere became heated, and the whole country of the desert, which was once a sea whose waters cooled the air of the countries round it, was apparently but a vast expanse where heat sprang from the very soil.

I took refuge at length in St. Louis, where the houses are made of stone, and, like other people, I shut myself up in the house, and kept the windows and the doors closed, so that no hot air could come in. In this way the houses are kept tolerably cool. For three days this terrible weather lasted, except that the nights were somewhat cooler. These hot winds from the desert often blow two or three days at a time, and sometimes last a whole week, bringing with them disease and death to the white man.

When, perchance, I would come out of the place where I had to shut myself up, I felt the hot wind blowing in my face, and breathed this heated atmosphere with a feeling that it was gradually killing me. What must it be then, I thought, in the desert, far from the sea and from rivers! There life must be sometimes almost unbearable. In certain seasons of the year these hot winds blow quite frequently, and sometimes only a few hours a day. Fortunately, the people living by the sea-shore do not suffer from them as much as the people of the interior.

If you had called on me during this hot weather, my dear young folks, you would have probably been astonished to see the way I would have received you, and the queer manner in which I held my reception, inviting my guests to do the same as I did; but, in order to give you an idea of this, I must explain how water is kept in that part of the world.

The dry season in Senegal lasts about eight months. The white people, during the rainy season, collect all the water they can, either in cisterns, or in immense earthen jars, some of which are so large that a man can go into them through the opening. These jars are manufactured in Marseilles, and some of them must hold fifty or sixty gallons, and even more. The water is kept in them deliciously cool. A very fat man could not get in one of these jars, as the opening is small compared with the body.

In one of my rooms I had several of these jars, in some of which I kept a little water, while in others I kept none. When the terrible hot weather came, it struck me that the coolest place I could find was inside of one of these jars, as they were very thick, and not liable to become heated through. So I made the trial, and found the experiment worked to a charm, and that I had discovered a cool retreat. As soon as the desert wind began blowing, I would quietly put myself in one of these jars, and stay there for a few hours. When my friends were too stout to follow my example, I would apologize to them, and give the excuse that I had the largest jars that were made. Then my fat friend would look curiously at me, and say, "I wish I was as slender as you are."

The first time I tried the jars I had a great deal of fun. Somebody came to see me, and was sent into my room; but, in the mean time, having heard him coming,

I had drawn my head inside, and so remained perfectly concealed. Seeing nothing but jars, my visitor went into the next room, and, seeing nobody there, he shouted, "Where are you?" I answered back, still keeping my head below the opening, "Here I am!" He came back into my room and began to be bewildered. I could stand it no longer, and, bursting out with a loud laugh, showed my head above the jar-opening, and invited him to follow my example and "take a jar."

STRANGE RECEPTION.

During these hot spells the visitor would generally come in, feeling quite prostrated by the dry heat; and, after the usual salutation of "How do you do, sir?" the conversation would generally take the following turn:

"How is the weather outside?"

"Terribly hot, sir; suffocating; the scorching wind is

almost unbearable. The thermometer yesterday and to-day stood between one hundred and fifteen and one hundred and twenty."

"This is terrible, sir."

"Yes, sir; this is terrible."

"Won't you take off your coat, sir, and get in? I think you are not too large to get into one of these big jars. They are quite cool and comfortable, as the pottery is quite thick, and is glazed. There is a stool; step on it; it will make it more easy for you. If you are afraid the jar will tumble down, I will call somebody to help you. Two jars have water in, sir. Two are without. Take either one you like best."

Then, if the visitor was happy enough not to be too stout, he would, immediately after being bottled up, or rather, I should say, jarred up, shout, "How nice it is! How cool and pleasant! It is perfectly delightful! What a glorious idea! It is a good thing for you to be so slender!"

If the visitor was too fat to enter the jars, his first recognition of me would be that of wonder. Then he would come and examine the aperture of the jar, look at his body, and then give a tremendous sigh, and exclaim, "How unfortunate it is for a man to be too stout!"

CHAPTER XXVI.

WAITING FOR A START. — THREE YOUNG LIONS. — I PLAY WITH THEM. — HOW THEY WERE CAPTURED. — TERRIBLE COMBAT WITH THE LION AND THE LIONESS. — THEY ARE BOTH KILLED.

Having but little time to spare in Senegal, I wanted to make the most of it while there, and was waiting anxiously for a caravan that should leave for some part of the desert, in order to go with it.

While waiting for the opportunity, I would sometimes amuse myself with the three young lions that were in the village, and had a good deal of fun with them. Each lion had a name, which I wish I could remember. All I can say is, that they were real difficult names to pronounce, for the language of the people is hard and guttural. They were very tame, and as playful as young dogs; but, though young, they were much larger than any dog I ever saw.

I would go and play with them every morning, and sometimes during the day, but I always liked to go after they had had their meals. They knew exactly the time these were coming, and, for almost an hour before, they were too busy thinking about their breakfast or dinner to be playful. I must say I did not like to venture near them when they were in such a mood; for, though very tame, and though they had never bitten any body, yet they might have tried it on me for the first time. Their jaws were quite powerful, and I had strong doubts whether I should have come safely out of them had they once fastened on me.

They were also armed with somewhat powerful claws, which certainly could have torn my flesh with the greatest ease. I have no doubt that, as soon as they saw the blood flow, their natural instinct would have come back, and they would have pounced upon me. The sight of warm blood from the body would have awakened all their dormant feeling, if hungry. Even without going so far as to fear that I might become a prey to their young ferocity, I knew that, judging by the pain a cat can inflict with her sharp claws, that the more powerful lions might prove to be very unpleasant playmates. At any rate, although the natives had assured me that their claws had been cut and that there was no danger, I had no desire to have them tried on me.

I noticed that whenever a goat came in sight their eyes would glare, and their tails would wag angrily, and it was very evident that the goats would stand a poor chance if these young beasts of prey had their own way.

After their meals I would sometimes seat myself among them, caress them, and scratch them. This they seemed to enjoy amazingly, and would look at me with their peculiar eyes, which have nothing unkind or treacherous in them when they are not hungry or angry. Their look contrasted strangely with that of the treacherous tiger or leopard.

I wanted to know how these lions had been captured. I wanted to hear the story of my three "friends," how they had been deprived of their freedom, and how they had lost their *papa* and *mamma*. I knew that they could

PLAYING WITH YOUNG LIONS.

not have been taken away easily, unless the "old folks" were out of the way on some excursion to get food for themselves and their young. At last my curiosity was satisfied, and their story was told me by the side of the young lions themselves. If they could have understood the speech, they would have known how they were made prisoners. They certainly could not recollect the incidents which led to their captivity, as they were too young at that time.

The man who told me the story was an old man with a very white beard. Before he began, several people came and seated themselves on the ground by our side. The old man then began as follows:

"A party of Moors were returning with their herds from the pastures, which the heat had dried up. They were going to the southern part of the desert, where water was not so scarce, and where the grass was still fresh and sweet. The heads of the party were riding on camels. At length they came to an oasis, chiefly composed of dates and palm-trees. On reaching it they found evidences that lions were accustomed to go there, and, as there was a spring there, they concluded the beasts had come to drink.

"That day, with their large herd of cattle, they encamped by that oasis. Their beasts could satisfy their thirst at the spring, and eat of the grass in the surrounding country that was not quite parched up.

"At night the roar of lions that were lurking round told them that they must keep a strict watch over their cattle and horses. Fires were lighted with branches from the stunted trees, and throughout the night the people shouted, and now and then fired guns, to frighten the lions away; but, despite of all their care, one cow was carried off by the king of the desert.

"The next day the party of herdsmen moved again in a more southern direction; but four of the most daring Moors resolved to remain behind and see if they could not kill the lions, lest they might follow their track and destroy some of their cattle. These Moors belonged to the Trazas tribe, and among them was a young man who was very ambitious to be enrolled among their great warriors. As he had neither slain a lion nor an enemy in battle, he could not be so called, according to the custom of the tribe.

"So the herd moved on, and the rest of the people with them; but our four Trazas remained behind, and all that day were busy looking for traces of the lions. They were armed, like all the Trazas, with double-barreled flint guns, pistols, and huge knives. After searching many hours in vain, they came to a thicket of trees, which they entered cautiously, mistrusting that lions might be hidden there. Suddenly they saw three young cubs playing together, though no old lions were to be seen. No doubt the old folks had gone to visit the carcass of the cow they had killed the day before, for the purpose of bringing food home to their youngsters.

"Looking carefully to their guns, in order to be ready for any thing that might happen, two of them descended from their camels, seized the young lions, and remounted with their game, handing the third cub to one of their companions. They then left with the utmost speed their camels could make, for their only safety was to be out of the reach of the lions' pursuit when they should come back and find their young taken away. Their rage would be terrific, and woe to the men who had dared to take their young. Of course they had guns, and would try to kill the lions if attacked, but it would be a dangerous business. So on they went, now and then looking behind to see if the lions were after them. Never did their camels go so fast before.

"They had been gone about two hours, and began to think themselves safe, when, to their horror, looking back on reaching an open country, they saw the lion and lioness in hot pursuit. They urged their camels on as fast as they could, but gradually the lions gained upon them, until their roars of rage could be distinctly heard. Nearer and nearer the pursuers came, till at last the Moors saw it was of no use to attempt to escape by running away, and that they must prepare for a fight if they wanted to get clear with their lives. In the mean time, two of the young cubs had been securely tied in a kind of basket or bag.

"They agreed that, as soon as the lions should come near enough, they would throw off one of the young cubs to distract the attention of the lioness. At the same time one of them would fire at the lion, and, if he was not killed by the shot, another would fire at him again. As they were all good marksmen, they were very hopeful to be able to kill them.

"The lions came roaring and bounding on, and one of the young ones was thrown down to the lioness, who immediately stopped to caress it, while her mate continued the chase. As he sprang forward in the air, one of the young Moors fired at him. The bullet took effect, and the huge beast, giving a tremendous roar of pain, rolled over in the sand, the blood pouring from his wound in a torrent. Another bullet went into his massive forehead, and, giving utterance to a most appalling and terrific roar, he rolled over and died. The lioness was then dispatched by two or three well-aimed shots, and the cub was recaptured without difficulty.

"In this way," added the old man, in conclusion, "these young lions were taken, and afterward sold to us by the Trazas people. We have brought them up in our village, and intend to sell them after a while."

CHAPTER XXVII.

DEPARTURE.—A CARAVAN.—APPEARANCE OF THE PEOPLE. —RIDING A CAMEL.—I AM CAMEL-SICK.—WELLS IN THE SAND.

I WAS obliged to wait so long for a caravan that I began to feel somewhat fearful that I should have to leave the Senegal country without a visit to the Great Desert; but at last the opportunity arrived. An excursion was arranged with which I was to go, which would at least take me to the borders of the Sahara. While waiting for my companions to get ready, I usually employed my afternoons in walking along the shore till I came to a spot where nothing was before me but the ocean sparkling in the sunlight. Not a soul was ever within sight. Behind me lay an ocean of barren sand, so loose that it was most difficult and fatiguing to walk through it. How strangely the wind whispered as it blew from that immense extent of scorching desert! The landscape was gloomy and forlorn, and had a most depressing influence over me. Between the sad murmurs of the wind, and the solemn and monotonous noise of the waves as they broke on the shore, I could not tell which was the most melancholy sound to hear. But still I loved to seat myself on the edge, if I may so term it, of the Great Desert, and have before me the wide Atlantic; for then thoughts of home would come over me, and many memories of the dear friends I had left behind.

A CARAVAN OF MOORS.

At last, when my patience was almost exhausted, the preparations for our trip were finished, and the day of departure came. The caravan was going somewhere far to the north, and was to follow the line of the sea-shore; and it was arranged that a certain number of men were to remain with me whenever I chose to stay behind for the purpose of hunting, for I did not intend to go with them to the end of their journey. I only wanted to enjoy the novelty of real desert-life for a little while.

The men were mounted on a great variety of animals, camels, horses, and donkeys; and when offered my choice, I selected a camel, having never ridden one in my life. Every man was armed with a double-barreled flint-lock gun, and some had pistols and swords. The party was accompanied by a marabout (Mohammedan priest); he was a strange-looking old man, with a white beard, and seemed to be very much venerated by the people.

We had with us all that was necessary for a camp. Our tents were made of the coarse cotton cloth manufactured by the people, and for beds we had soft tanned leather mats. For myself, I had bought a splendid rug, made by the Moors, exceedingly soft, the material of which was young calves' skins.

One splendid morning, immediately after our Mohammedan priest had recited his prayers, we set out, and I must say that there was something very picturesque in our departure. The men all wore broad-brimmed hats and loose barbaric costumes; some were mounted on small, hardy donkeys, others on horses, and a very few on camels. Other beasts were loaded with provisions and goods which were to be taken to the Moors.

My camel was made to kneel down by his master to

enable me to climb upon his back. I was told that he was very gentle and docile. I must have looked queer enough with that immense straw hat on my head, my double-barreled gun over my shoulder, my pistols hanging by my side, and a huge hunting-knife, as sharp almost as a razor, the bright steel of which shone splendidly as the rays of the sun struck upon it.

A camel-saddle is a queer-looking affair, and as for the riding, I must say I did not like the camel's jolting gait very much.

Our road lay along the barren and shadeless sea-shore, and gradually the sun reminded me that the day was advancing, and that it was getting hot. The glare on the white sand and the reflection from the sea were very painful to the eyes, and I did not wonder that ophthalmy was so prevalent among the people there. It became positively unbearable as the day wore on, in despite of my big broad-brimmed hat, and at length I put over my face a very thick green veil with which I had happily provided myself, and for which I was very thankful. After riding some time I began to feel a queer sensation in my stomach. The long, swinging strides of my camel, to which, of course, I was not accustomed, did not seem to agree with me, and I was beginning to feel symptoms of sea-sickness. "What," said I to myself, "sea-sick on the back of a camel?" There was no mistake about it. It was a kind of camel-sickness. The men had a good laugh at me; but I tried to fight it down, and after a while succeeded, just as I was on the point of giving up friend camel and betaking myself to the back of a high-spirited donkey, on which I had fixed my eyes before we started. He was a beauty of his kind; but I was told that he was a very obstinate creature when he took it into his head to be so. After all, I did not find that my camel was such a gentle and docile animal as I had been told. I thought it was pretty obstinate.

By noon the air became very hot, and the sand was so scorching that it would have been no fun to walk through it barefooted. We were going very slowly, and toward four o'clock we thought we would pitch our tents and encamp for the night. A spot by the sea-shore was chosen for a site, and then the people began to busy themselves in digging holes in the sand about high-water mark. I did not know at first what they were doing this for, but soon discovered that they were digging wells. These were six or seven feet in diameter, and, as the sand was very loose, the workmen were constantly hindered by the caving in of the sides; but, in spite of this drawback, the wells in a short time were completed to a depth of about six feet, when water began to show itself, as they had dug below the level of the sea. In two wells the water was brackish, while in two others it tasted quite fresh and sweet. We kept one for ourselves, and made the approach to the other accessible for our beasts. The poor creatures, suffering from thirst, came and drank so greedily that twice they had to be driven back to let the water come in again, they having completely emptied the well.

These rude wells are very useful, and, if properly protected by iron tubes, would be of immense benefit. This manner of digging wells is the usual method of getting water by the sea-shore.

Mohammedans are always very devout, and a little before sunset all the people became quiet, and listened reverently while the marabout prayed aloud. Afterward they seated themselves cross-legged on the sand, with their faces turned toward the setting sun, saying their evening prayer to Allah, whose sole prophet they believed to be Mohammed. Then the camels and other animals, so tethered as to prevent their straying far from camp, were turned loose to graze on the scanty herbage that grew here and there along the shore. The evening meal was eaten with good appetite, and after this important duty was dispatched I took a solitary stroll along the beach to watch the camels feeding. As I observed these faithful, patient, and docile creatures, I could not help thinking how bountiful and wonderful is Nature in providing for man's wants in the different countries of the world. Every where animals are found adapted for the mode of life required according to the formation and climate of the country. In desert and arid lands, where food is scarce, and even water is far from being abundant, the camel is found, and proves to be the best friend of man. Not only can this animal go several days without drinking as it crosses the great Sahara, but the milk of the female camel furnishes her master with drink. Many a wanderer's life has been saved in that manner. As for food, the camel will be satisfied with the parched grass, the scraggy vines, or the dry branches of the stunted trees found in the desert, or a few handfuls of grain or dry dates. I do not wonder that the natives love their camels, for what would they do in that desert country without them?

How is it that the camel, unlike other animals, can go so long a time without drinking water? I will tell you. In its stomach are a great number of deep cells into which the water passes when the camel drinks, and is then prevented from escaping by a muscle which closes the mouth of the cells. When the camel feels thirsty, it has the power of using some of this reserved store of water. The natives say that when a camel has been accustomed to a certain route, he knows exactly how long to keep this supply of water to make it last from one well or spring to another. Hence there is sometimes danger of a camel's suffering from thirst, and even dying, if a long journey is to be performed over a route with which he is unacquainted. The camel's feet are broad, and so constructed that they present a broad surface to the desert sands, to prevent his sinking into it too deeply. Their knees are hard and horny, from the habit of kneeling down to be loaded and unloaded.

The Moors come frequently down to the banks of the Senegal River with an imposing array of camels, loaded with gum arabic. The sight of one of these caravans is curious and picturesque, as may be seen by the illustration on another page.

CHAPTER XXVIII.

PART WITH THE CARAVAN.—A NEW CAMP.—DISCOVER OSTRICH TRACKS.—AN OSTRICH'S NEST.—AN OMELETTE.—CHASING OSTRICHES ON HORSEBACK.—I AM UNSUCCESSFUL.—LARGE NUMBER OF SEA-SHELLS IN THE DESERT.

When I came out of my tent early the next morning, I saw the Mohammedans scattered all over the sand round our encampment, with their faces turned toward the rising sun, saying their morning prayers before the start. Then the camels and asses were milked, they were fed with grain, and then led to the wells to drink. Breakfast over, then we started on our way again. That day I was to be left by the caravan, for they did not wish to take me farther, on account of the unsafe condition of the country northward. The plundering Moors were roving about in strong bands, and frequently attacked caravans after dark.

I was overjoyed to find evidences that ostriches had been in the region through which we passed. This assured me that there was to be good sport in the Sahara, and not far from the sea.

Late in the afternoon I took leave of the caravan. Several donkeys and a fleet horse were left for my use. After many a good-by we parted, and I remained with a few splendid Jaloffs for companions. We built our camp near a scrubby grove, and dug a well, finding pretty good water at a depth of six feet. During the night we kept a very careful watch lest the plunderers of the desert should surprise us. The Moors might capture and make me a slave—I, who love to be free! What should I do if I was to lose my freedom? I shudder at the thought! I would rather die, I said to myself, than suffer such a terrible fate; and then the story of the poor wretched men who had been taken captives on the coast, which I have told you in a former chapter, came into my mind. You will not be surprised to learn that I slept but little that night. Fortunately, nothing happened to disturb us.

In the morning, after a hearty breakfast, I began hunting on the country back of the spot where we had encamped. I had to be very careful, and keep a sharp lookout, as sometimes lions were found in these regions. I was after ostriches, and had not gone far from our camp with my four companions, when we discovered fresh tracks, which must have been made by these singular birds but a short time before. Among the scanty shrubs thereabout were some creeping vines, which bore a kind of fruit upon which the ostriches had been feeding. I was on the alert, but the ground was flat, and there was little probability of my getting near the birds, as they could see me, and run away. Their swiftness is almost incredible, for they have most extraordinary muscular power in their legs, and, though they can not soar into the air, their wings assist them wonderfully in their flight.

I could not understand at first how these ostriches had strayed into this region, and finally concluded that they must have been driven from the north by hunters, and had taken refuge here. But there was no mistake about it; my guide said the footprints were really made by ostriches. I therefore continued my chase till I came unawares upon an ostrich nest, which was a piece of very good fortune for me. It was not built of straw nor dead branches, but was simply a hole scooped out in the sand by the mother bird. I was glad to observe that there were five in the nest, which, if they were fresh, would make a fine omelette. Satisfied with our good luck, and considerably tired with the long tramp over the sandy plain, we concluded to return to camp with our five eggs. They were quite a nice little load.

Our camp was somewhat sheltered from the fresh sea-breeze by a little sand-hillock heaped together by the action of the wind. The broad Atlantic was before us, and the waves came dashing heavily on the beach. In the evening the sky was clear, and the stars shone out most beautifully. We had no matting, our bed being nothing but the white desert sand, and a very nice and comfortable bed it made, I can assure you.

When we were comfortably settled, I said to Mokar Sidi, "Bring us the frying-pan. I must have an omelette made of an ostrich egg." But what a big omelette it was going to be, for the capacity of an ostrich egg is about thirty times that of a hen's egg. I wondered if the omelette would be good. One thing was certain, the egg was newly laid. We had with us a large quantity of butter, which was carefully kept in a leather bag. I had my frying-pan—a large tin plate—and was ready to begin.

The shell of the ostrich egg was rather thick, and it required two or three good blows with my hunting-knife to break it. The contents of the egg half filled quite a large dish. I beat it with my fork for a long time, till the yellow and the white were thoroughly mixed. Then I put the pan on the bright fire we had built with pieces of wood collected from the shrubs around our camp. I melted about a pound of butter, and, while it was very hot, mixed the egg and the butter thoroughly with a spoon. With the addition of salt and pepper, the omelette was soon ready, and such an omelette as it was! It would have done you good to see it. I am sure it would have given you a keen appetite. It looked and tasted very much like an ordinary omelette. It was somewhat coarser in flavor, but nourishing; and, as it was the first time in my life I tasted of an ostrich-egg omelette, I relished it very much. Most of my fellows made their supper on couscous, a kind of millet, but some of them had a dish of pounded grasshoppers. Among the children of the desert this is considered a great dainty, and I was told the Moors are also very fond of it.

As I wished to carry home the rest of the eggs, I made a hole in one end of each, through which I emptied the contents. The natives sometimes use these egg-shells to hold water, or cut them up into spoons, dishes, cups, and other articles of household convenience. One of these eggs will hold about three pints.

The following day, before sunrise, while walking near the camp, I spied two ostriches in the distance, too far off to be conscious of my presence. I went back into my tent as quickly as I could, and saddled and mounted my horse, and started quietly in pursuit, taking every advantage of the ground as I advanced, in order not to be seen by the game.

I felt somewhat anxious about my riding qualities, for I knew I was not at all a good horseman, but I had the consolation of knowing that if I fell off it would be upon the soft sand, for there were no rocks on which I should break my head. After this reflection, I started on a tremendous gallop after the ostriches. My little horse went on splendidly, and we gained rapidly on them. There was a fair prospect, I thought, for me to bag one, when, just as I was ready to cock my gun, down I fell at full length on the sand! My gun pitch-

AN OSTRICH HUNT.

ed a long way ahead of me, and my mouth was filled up with sand. I gathered myself up, and, finding that there were no bones broken, picked up my gun and started in pursuit of my horse. He was a gentle and well-trained animal, and suffered himself to be caught without difficulty.

The game, by that time, were far away, and I returned to the camp, promising myself not to go after ostriches on horseback again, or, at any rate, not before I had a little more practice in riding.

The ostrich does not run so fast as people generally suppose; at least they can not run a long distance, and a horse can easily overtake them, in spite of their legs and wings. The natives say they can kick tremendously, and that dogs are often killed in that way, as the powerful sharp claw with which the foot is armed can make fearful wounds.

The male is a splendid bird; the lower part of the neck and the body is of a beautiful shiny black, and the plumes of the wing and tail are white. The female is of a grayish-brown color, sprinkled with white, and her tail and wing-plumes are clear white. The male possesses the finest feathers. They are from six to eight feet in height, and the body weighs probably from two to three hundred pounds.

I returned to camp somewhat crestfallen in regard to riding. The least agreeable part of all had been that I got my mouth full of sand, and could not get rid of it till I came back to the camp, where I could rinse it out with water.

I was surprised at the number of sea-shells scattered about in the sands of the desert, showing conclusively to my mind that once this barren and scorching expanse had been covered by a sea. As the level of the desert is not much above that of the ocean, I feel certain that if wells were dug all over the desert, and protected with iron tubes to prevent the sands from falling in, water could be easily supplied to caravans and bands of travelers in their journeys across that terrible expanse of territory.

CHAPTER XXIX.

A SAND-STORM PREDICTED.—THE WIND FROM THE NORTHEAST.—THE STORM.—AFTER OSTRICHES.—TWO ARE KILLED.—RETURN TO CAMP.—ROAST OSTRICH FOR SUPPER.—RETURN TO THE SETTLEMENT.

On my return to the camp the men said we were going to have a storm from the desert. They could tell it was coming, and they hoped it would not last long, for these storms are very unpleasant. They did not mean a storm of rain, but that a strong wind would blow from the east or northeast, and, in passing over the Great Desert, would raise clouds and columns of sand, so that the atmosphere would be thick with it, as if a fog had spread itself over the country.

I may say I was glad to hear this. Like you, my dear young folks, I had heard before of these sand-storms, and that the sand would even be carried far away out to sea and fall on the decks of ships. I wanted to see one of these awful storms, which are said to be so violent in the Great Desert that men, and sometimes caravans, are buried alive beneath the immense masses of sand.

The men were not mistaken. The wind, which had been blowing lightly in an east-northeast direction, began to increase gradually, till at last it blew a perfect gale. The sand began to fly, and the storm increased still more. The air soon became murky with sand, which flew to-

SAND-STORM IN THE DESERT.

ward the sea like a thick fog. It was a grand and splendid sight. The light of the day had become quite dim, because the sun's rays could hardly pierce the clouds of sand. It continued blowing for several hours. The wind was hot; my lips became parched and my eyes sore, as, in spite of my thick veil, the sand penetrated every where. Now that I had seen a genuine sand-storm, I hoped that the wind would moderate. Little hillocks and mounds were formed here and there, and our wells were filled up with the drifting sand.

The sand got into my clothes through every opening in them. It filled my hair, my nose, my ears, and even my mouth. It covered every thing in our camp, and completely spoiled our food. But we had to eat it as it was, as there was no choice.

Toward evening the wind gradually calmed down, and by the time the sun had set below the horizon nature became quiet again. The sand-storm of the desert was over, and I was glad I had seen it.

The next morning I again prepared myself to hunt the ostrich. Some of them had been seen the day before by some of the men who had wandered off a little way into the desert. It was but seldom that ostriches were seen where we were, and I wished to take advantage of the opportunity, the more so that I should have to turn back very soon and leave the Senegal region for the Gulf of Guinea.

But first we moved our camp a few miles northward from where we were, because better wells of water could be got in that locality. As soon as our tents were pitched again, I started once more on an ostrich hunt, taking two guides with me.

Our course lay through the desert near the sea-shore. It was exceedingly tiresome walking, for at every step we made our feet would go deep into the sand, and the heat was intense. We had to take every advantage of the ground in order to hide ourselves from sight, for the ostriches, as you know, were very shy, and, though I had been more than three hours on the way, and was assured by my two guides that I should see some, I was yet to discover the first one. I did not expect to see their tracks, as the storm of the day before had obliterated every trace of them.

Yet I had good reason to look for fine sport, for this was the time—just at the close of May, and before the setting in of the rainy season—when the ostriches are accustomed to visit the sea-shore in great numbers. The natives say they wade into the sea during the heat of the day, and splash round in the water at a great rate. This, as you may suppose, is the best time of the year to shoot them.

All at once, as I reached the top of a sand-down or hill, I looked carefully over the crest to see if I could discern any signs of game, and, to my great delight, I saw several ostriches near the sea-shore, and not far from where I was posted. I instantly stopped, and stood still for an instant to observe them. I had never seen them in their wild state till the day previous, and was very much interested in watching their movements as they were strutting about on the shore.

After satisfying my curiosity, I crept toward them with all the caution I could use. They were unaware of my presence, and seemed to be perfectly unconcerned about every thing around them; but, knowing how keen their scent was, I advanced cautiously and slowly, reserving my fire until I came within very short range. If you had been with me you would have become, I am sure, quite as much excited as I was, and you would have enjoyed the chase.

At last I came to a gap between two sand-hills, which put me in great anxiety, as there was danger of my being discovered by the ostriches in crossing, and if I should be, good-by to my hopes! The gap was about forty yards wide, and I must cross it in the quickest and most sly manner. So, protected behind a little hillock of sand, I watched carefully for a chance to scud across. My eyes were riveted on the ostriches, and I waited for a time till they should all look toward the sea or go into the surf, so that I could shift my position without being seen,

AFTER OSTRICHES.

and gain a hillock that stood within easy range of my beautiful game. At last a good chance came; they all clustered together and turned their backs toward me, looking in the opposite direction. I seized the opportunity, and crossed over the open space in a jiffy, never letting my eyes lose sight of the ostriches, so that if they had suddenly looked back I should have thrown myself flat in the sand and lain as still as a log or a stone. Using all this caution, I crossed in safety, and, on reaching the other shelter, drew a long breath of relief. I was within range of the ostriches at last, and sure of my game.

I rested several seconds in order to get breath to calm my nerves, so that I might take good aim and make a dead shot. Then I slowly raised my gun, took a steady aim at the male, who led the flock, and pulled the trigger. Bang! down came the male ostrich. Bang again! and down came another. The three others that remained alive fled with very great swiftness. This was great sport. I had been entirely successful. I gave a wild shout of joy, and my two friends, who had remained behind, and were watching my movements, ran toward me as fast as they could. I sent one of them back to the camp to fetch the other men to assist in carrying the game. The beautiful feathers were pulled out, the ostriches were cut into small pieces, and then, singing songs of triumph, we returned to camp. That evening we had a splendid supper of roast ostrich.

The next day I thought it was time to go back, for the vessel was soon to be ready to sail, and I must reluctantly say good-by to the Great Desert. So we raised our camp, loaded our donkeys, and departed on our homeward way. It was with a feeling of sorrow that I said good-by to these desert and sandy shores, where I had really enjoyed myself, and learned something that I did not know before.

A few days after my return to the settlement of St. Louis we weighed anchor and sailed for the Gulf of Guinea.

CHAPTER XXX.

A PLEASANT VOYAGE.—IN SIGHT OF THE CAMEROONS.—THE ISLAND OF FERNANDO PO.—SHARKS.—THE PILOT-FISH.—WHAT THEY DO.—HOOKING OF A BIG SHARK.—ITS STRUGGLES.—ITS DEATH.

For a few days after getting under way we had a light breeze, and then sailed into the region of calms, where vessels are sometimes detained for weeks for want of wind enough to fill their canvas. We were not so unfortunate, however, and thirty-eight days after our departure from Senegal our ship was plowing through the water finely. We had a nice breeze, all our sails were set, and the studding-sails were out. As I looked back one morning, I could see our wake for a long distance. The sun had risen half an hour before, and the deck had just been washed. I was enjoying the coolness of a morning at sea under the tropics. The captain was smoking a pipe as hard as he could. I could see that he was nervous and excited. The fact was that he had been expecting to see the land at sunrise, and had been disappointed. He concluded that the strong currents had thrown us northward.

One man had been sent to the top of the mainmast to watch for the land, for of course he could see it from such a height long before those who were on deck.

The captain and I were talking of the strength of the

currents, and wondering how far we might be out of our course, when suddenly the cry of "Land ahead! land ahead!" came down to us from the man on the watch at the top of the mainmast. Immediately the captain and I took our spy-glasses and ascended the rigging, though I was satisfied not to go as high as the captain. The fact was that I did not care to go higher up, not being much of a sailor, and not knowing how I should like it up there, or how I should keep my footing. I had no idea of trying, for I knew that if I did not succeed I should have a terrible fall. While I was thinking of these things, the captain looked down and said to me, "Do not go up higher." I was only too ready to obey. After looking a while through my glass, I shouted to him, "Land ahead! land ahead!" The captain said, "Where?" I pointed toward the land, and said, "Don't you see it there?" I could not be mistaken. What I saw could not be a cloud, though it looked very much like one, so faint and very far away. All I could see above the sea was an indistinct bluish mass, having the appearance of a cloud or bank of mist; but there was a hazy atmosphere about it which looked very much as if it were land. As we came near it became more substantial, and at last the blue outlines of the great peak of Cameroons were seen. What a grand sight it presented! apparently rising like an island from the sea, for the country that surrounds it is low and marshy, and the peak, which rises to a height of thirteen thousand feet above the sea, is visible for several hours before the low lands above which it towers come into sight.

I wondered if this Peak of Cameroons was the same land which Hanno, the great Carthaginian admiral, mentions in the Periplus, where he says: "We discovered, at night, a country full of fire. In the middle was a lofty fire, larger than all the rest, which seemed to touch the stars. When day came we discovered it to be a large hill, called Teonochema, the Chariot of the Gods."

The Cameroons Mountains, being of volcanic origin, would seem to corroborate this theory. Extinct craters are to be seen there which must have been for ages in a state of repose, and there is no other spot on the West Coast where remains of volcanoes can be seen.

Hanno, if you remember well, mentions also the gorilla in the same book.

At a distance the Cameroons seems to rise abruptly from its base by a continuous slope; but, on nearer approach, it is seen to consist of a succession of hills and valleys, covered with alternating forest and pasture land. Perhaps one third is covered with dense forest, while the summit is bare.

After a few hours the island of Fernando Po, whose peaks rise to a height of more than ten thousand feet, was in sight, and we could see, at the same time, the two highest points found on the West Coast of Africa, for Fernando is only about twenty miles from the main land. It is situated in the very Bight of Biafra, which is the extreme end of the Gulf of Guinea. One of the affluents of the great River Niger here falls into the sea.

While our vessel was heading for Fernando Po, I was seated near the rudder, looking now and then at the high land of which I have just spoken, when suddenly I saw the fins of a large shark in the water. By their size it must have been an enormous creature. It seemed to be hunting after fish, as it swam pretty fast. No doubt the shark was hungry. I threw something heavy in the water, which made a good deal of splashing, to attract its attention. I was not mistaken. The huge fish made for the vessel, swam round it, though we were sailing fast, and then came back to the stern, and followed us closely. Sometimes it almost seemed as if it touched the rudder. What a huge creature it was! how ugly, how voracious! Its little eyes seemed to see every thing; but its mouth could not be seen, for it is placed in such a way that it can only be seen when the shark turns over. I wondered how many rows of teeth the creature could have, and a cold shudder ran over me; for just at that time I had seated myself on the bulwarks of the vessel, and the least jerk might have sent me over into the sea, and, as the shark was swimming close to the vessel, there would have been no way of escape. I immediately jumped down on deck and looked at the creature. I do not wonder that the natives often call it the "leopard of the sea," for such a voracious creature seldom can be met any where. You may perhaps remember that in "Lost in the Jungle" there is an eagle called by the people "the leopard of the air" on account of its fierceness and boldness. The water has its representative for voracity, fierceness, and treachery in the shark, and the land has the leopard, which, as the natives say, can not be trusted.

As I was looking at that shark, I saw eight little fish swimming round it, on which the shark seemed to look complacently. At first I wondered why the shark did not gobble them up as he would other fish. Now these little tiny things would seem to rest on the back of their huge companion, then they would swim under its belly and round him. As I watched these little creatures, I was filled with wonder because they swam so fast. They seemed to be his best friends, and, as I learned, are called the shark's pilots, and follow him every where. Only large sharks have pilots. Wherever the shark goes his "little pilots" follow him. I believe they sometimes tell him of danger, for the great enemy of the shark is the "sawfish." At any rate, they never leave the shark, and it may be that they help to keep its skin clear from insects and parasites. I went to my stateroom, and took from a box two or three very small fish-hooks, which I tied to a thread, and then put a very small piece of fat pork on the hook, and dropped it in the water, but the little pilots would not bite.

At times I fancied the old big shark was looking at me, hoping all the time that I would come down into the water, when he would have made a jolly meal of me.

At last I gave up trying to catch the little pilot-fish. It is not often that I give up, but I saw that in this case it was of no use, for it did not even come and smell of my bait. Whatever little things I would throw over, such as crusts of bread, little pieces of chicken-meat, etc., they would not trouble themselves in the least about; so I came to the conclusion that they fed themselves on the parasites of the shark.

Just as I was thinking of catching the big shark, the bell for dinner rang, and I went down into the cabin in a hurry, for I was very hungry. A piece of salt pork and some beans was all we had for our dinner. I confess I should have willingly exchanged the salt pork for something else, for we had had so much of it.

After dinner I went immediately on deck again, and saw that the shark was still following the vessel. The sailor at the wheel whispered to me, in a very low tone, that one of the crew was sick, and that he had no doubt that the shark was waiting for him to die; "for," added the sailor, "those horrid creatures smell sickness on board, and I have seen them follow a ship day after day till the man died and his body was buried in the sea." Almost every sailor believes what this man just told me, and that it is always a bad sign to see a shark follow after a sick man. I said, "Nonsense; I do not believe a word about it. You sailors are full of superstitions. At any rate, I am going to try to hook the 'fellow,' so that it shall be his last day in the sea." We had on board the vessel two large fish-hooks, which I had got specially for shark fishing. These big hooks were held by a chain about eighteen inches long, for a rope would have stood a poor chance against several rows of teeth.

As I was preparing my hook and was ready to put on it a piece of pork which weighed about one pound, the captain came and helped me. We attached to the chain a new, strong rope, for the shark was a big one, and we secured it to the deck. The vessel was not going at that time more than three miles an hour, for the breeze had become light; but we were going fast enough. The hook, with its piece of pork as a bait, had hardly dropped into the water, when the shark came at it, and suddenly turned over on its back, and showed a tremendous mouth, which it opened, and swallowed pork, fish-hook, and part of the chain. We gave a sudden jerk to our line, and the hook fastened itself tightly inside the jaw of Master Shark. Then came a great struggle to haul him up, especially when we got him out of the water and against the ship's side. The crew had to be called to assist us before we succeeded in landing him on the deck. It was all that eight men could do to pull him up. Now and then his powerful tail would strike with terrific force against the sides of the ship; the water was lashed into foam, and was soon discolored with blood from the wound made by the hook. At last we succeeded in drawing it out of the water, and the little pilot-fish swam about at random, not knowing where their protector and friend had disappeared. Then came the hardest part of the work, for the shark made a tremendous struggle, having no idea of being hauled on deck. Nevertheless, in spite of its desperate efforts, we succeeded. As soon as the huge creature fell on the deck we jumped out of its reach, for a single blow from its tail would have broken a man's leg. Now and then the shark would remain

CAPTURE OF A SHARK.

still a moment, then a quiver would follow, and the body would flop and twist till the strength of the monster appeared to be exhausted.

Finally it lay quite still. Having armed myself with a big axe belonging to the carpenter of the ship, I cut off the shark's tail with one blow. It was a monstrous shark. One of the sailors gave him a fearful blow on the head which almost split it in two. Even this rough treatment did not kill him, and it was still dangerous to approach within his reach. At length a powerful blow with an axe on the spine cut the monster in two and finished him, though the fragments of the body quivered for some time afterward.

This shark belonged to the most voracious species; it had a flat head, a big and very ugly-looking mouth, with several rows of teeth which looked like those of a wood-saw.

We had hardly killed this fellow than seven others appeared and followed in the wake of the ship. I threw overboard some pieces of the shark we had killed, upon which they threw themselves voraciously and gobbled them up. So they were cannibals, if we may use the expression, and, as the negroes say, they eat "their own people." They kept following the ship as if expecting that something more would be thrown over to them.

The thought came to my mind how dreadful it would be if one of the sailors should fall into the sea. It would be sure death to him, for the sharks would pounce upon him as the hungry and voracious hyena pounces upon a dead carcass. The captain seemed to have the same feeling, and, though such an accident hardly ever happens, he warned the men to look out sharp and be careful.

I was bound to kill these seven sharks if I could, for

if I succeeded there would be, I thought, seven monsters less in the sea—seven creatures that would never again make a meal of a man. So the two hooks were again put out with big pieces of pork upon them. They hardly touched the water when two sharks were caught, and, after a great struggle, but not so severe as that with the one we had just captured, they were hauled up half way, and then I put a bullet through the head of each, cut their tails off, and then let their bodies drop into the water; the five that remained pounced upon them with a fury and a voracity which astonished me. Of course, the sharks could not swim, their tails having been cut off, though they seemed to try. They sank gradually, the five sharks sinking with them into the depths of the ocean, to devour them. I did not count on that. It never entered my head that these would follow the disabled and half dead sharks in this manner.

Half an hour after another immense fellow made its appearance. We were decidedly in a great region of sharks. This fellow was a blue-skinned shark, long, and of slender proportions. The baited hook was thrown over to him, and he approached it slowly and with great caution, smelling at it three or four times, and as often rejecting it. He was certainly not very hungry; but at last he swallowed the bait and was caught. We had great work to bring him on deck. This monster was fourteen feet long, and you may judge my astonishment when I found that his stomach was filled with fish, some of which were still alive, and the captain had them broiled for his dinner. In the mean time we were getting nearer to the island of Fernando Po, and by sunset we were safely anchored in Clarence Bay, within twenty or thirty yards of the shore.

CHAPTER XXXI.

THE BOOBEES. — CAMP BY THE SEA. — WE SPY A CANOE. — FUGITIVES FROM SLAVERY. — THE STORY OF THEIR CAPTIVITY.—THEIR FLIGHT.

The next morning when I went on deck, the beautiful island rose before me in all its picturesque charms. Not a cloud hung over its high summit. The hills were covered with dense forest to their very tops, and from their gentle declivities numberless little rivulets ran sparkling down to the sea. The island is very beautiful to the eye, but very unhealthy for a residence.

There was at that time on the island a settlement of negroes captured from slavers, called Freetown, where several missionaries lived who had undertaken the care of the benighted people. The village was pretty and quite clean. Fruit-trees had been planted about the houses, and the little settlement appeared to be very thrifty. The island seemed to be under English rule, though belonging to Spain. A good, kind Hollander, who had been many years on the island, was the virtual governor.

Two or three days after my arrival, as I was rambling among the valleys and hills of the island, shooting birds and other small game (for, of course, there were no elephants nor leopards to be found, no hippopotami, etc., etc., there), I came across several settlements of the primitive inhabitants. These natives are called Boobees, and are, no doubt, the remnants of a powerful tribe which once inhabited the island. Strange to say, these Boobees are unlike the negroes of the main land, being far more ugly and degraded. They were accustomed to rub their bodies with clay and palm-oil mixed together, and many had a curious way of arranging their hair in plaits, each of which was stuck together with the same disgusting mixture in the shape of cigars. Some of them seemed to have hundreds of these cigar-shaped plaits or braids on their heads, sticking out on all sides like the quills on a porcupine.

Our camping-ground was situated in a nice little nook on the shore of one of those charming miniature bays which are found now and then along the coast of Fernando Po. Close beside it ran a beautiful little rivulet, the waters of which were as clear as crystal, and so cool that one might have been tempted to think that it came from some snowy peak. This little stream, indeed, rose in the mountains, and had meandered on its way to the sea through the dark forests of the island. Before us lay the sea. On the beach were two small canoes for fishing.

One morning when I returned from a hunt, in which I had succeeded in killing several squirrels, which were to be roasted that day on sticks, before a bright fire, for my dinner, and had stretched myself out on the sand under the protecting shade of some huge cotton-trees, I was looking at the water, and thinking that I would like, after a while, to go a-fishing. There was a lazy feeling in the atmosphere, and my men were taking their afternoon nap not far from where I was lying. I had been lying on the ground for about an hour, I suppose, when my attention was suddenly drawn to a black spot in the offing. What could it be? It was so far off that I took my spy-glass to examine it, and then discovered it was a small canoe, with a sail made of matting.

The little black spot grew bigger and bigger, for the wind was strong and from the sea. By the way the canoe sailed, I could see that the people wanted to make for the island. I wondered where the canoe could come from, and my curiosity was much excited; so I kept watching it as it came nearer and nearer, and after a while I could see that it contained five people. By the time it came within half a mile of the land, and was about that distance to the leeward of where our camp was, the breeze had gradually died away, and there was a dead calm. The canoe-men then took to their paddles, but, to my surprise, paddled very slowly. Examining them carefully through my glass, I recognized distinctly that there were four men and one woman in the canoe. They appeared to be emaciated, and, as they paddled very feebly, I concluded that they must be either sick or starving. Nevertheless, they were making headway. Who knows, said I to myself, but that it is a canoe belonging to the Boobees, which has been driven far out to sea by one of the fearful tornadoes which blow with such terrific force at this time of the year? I awoke my men, who immediately declared it was a canoe with fugitive slaves from Prince's or St. Thomas Island.

My sympathies were at once fully aroused, and I said, "Boys, suppose we launch one of our canoes and go to meet them?" "No," said my men; "for we might frighten them away." So I suggested that we should skirt the beach in the woods, and be near them when they landed. This was no sooner said than done, with all the more alacrity because the negroes forming my own camp were also fugitives from slavery. One of them, who had escaped from St. Thomas Island, and had lived on the banks of the Ogobai River, had been sold into slavery by his people because suspected of being a wizard. He had been three years in the English settlement of Fernando Po, and could speak the English language tolerably well, besides the Portuguese. His name was Fasiko.

We kept skirting the beach, taking good care to remain in the woods, in order not to raise the suspicions of the fugitives. By the time we came opposite them they were not more than one hundred yards from the shore. Through my glass I could see how careworn they were. They seemed to be very suspicious and shy as they approached the land, and I could see fear and anxiety on their faces. I was not surprised, for they had never seen the country, and knew not if the people were wicked and ready to kill them, or make slaves of them again. Now and then they would stop their paddles, look around anxiously, give two or three more strokes, then stop again, and look around. At last they landed, and appeared to be hardly able to walk. What a little bit of a canoe it was that they came in! I wondered that they had not been swamped.

After they had all landed, they looked carefully in every direction, while we kept ourselves hidden. Suddenly they saw human footsteps on the beach, where Boobees had been walking, and a kind of panic seized them.

Poor people! I felt sorry for them. At last my men came out of the forest, shouting to them not to be afraid; but the shouts were of no avail. They took to their heels and ran away as fast as they could; but, in their weakened condition, they were no match for us. We ran after them, and in a short time they were all captured. They immediately recognized friend Fasíko, however, who had lived on a neighboring plantation to theirs, and all at once their fears were allayed.

We took them back to the camp, and gave them a good meal of boiled plantains. Two chickens I had brought for myself were cooked for them, and the broth seemed to do them good. They were very grateful to us, and, after they had eaten, they lay down to seek the rest and sleep of which they stood so sadly in need. They were negroes from the interior of Africa, as we knew without being told by their sharp-pointed teeth and tattooed bodies.

Darkness had come, and we had given a fresh start to our fires, which were bright and cheerful, and our five runaway captives were lying by them with anxious looks, for they did not know what was to happen to them. Perhaps they thought I was one of the whites who bought slaves by the sea-shore, and that they were going to be re-enslaved.

"I want to hear your story," said I. "I want to know how you dared to go to sea in such a small canoe, and why you were sold into slavery by your own people." The eldest of the five rose from his reclining position, seated himself on the ground, and began to tell his story in Portuguese, which Fasiko translated into English.

"All of us you see here," said the old man, "belong

to a tribe called Ishogos, living far away from that big water" (he pointed to the sea), "of which we had never heard before we came to it, as none of those who go away from our country and see the ocean ever come back to tell the tale of what they have seen, for many tribes are between the ocean and our land; and, even if we escaped from the people of the coast, we should be enslaved by other tribes. A stranger in a strange land is not safe in the country of the black man." Here the man gave a sigh, and the others said, "*Yo, yo, yo,*" which meant "That is so."

"White man," he continued, "seest thou that woman? She lived in a village not far from mine. We grew up together. I saw her father and mother killed for witchcraft, and she saw my father and mother sold into slavery for the same cause; and, if we had dared to cry, or say that our parents were not sorcerers, we should have been killed, and therefore we were obliged to join the crowd, and shout with the rest of the people, 'Death to the wizards! Death to those who bring disease and death among us!' For, white man, in the country of the Ishogos, we all believe that people can become sorcerers; and if the people suspect that there are sorcerers in the village, we are afraid of each other, for we know not if our next neighbor does not wish to kill us. The father mistrusts his son, the son the father, the mother her children, the husband his wife, and the wife her husband, the uncle his nephew, and the nephew his uncle. Fear seizes every body, and there is no peace in the village till the sorcerers are found.

"So the people mistrusted us as belonging to a family of aniembas (sorcerers), and, as our people wanted brass rings, we were sold. In our country even mothers and fathers sell their own children, and our own family sold us into slavery. So one morning we left our village with a people called Apingi. They tied our hands behind our backs, and led us through the forest to their own country. This woman and I kept together. Oh how afraid we were of being separated; for when we were young we loved each other, and I wanted her to be my wife; but another man gave her father one slave more than I could afford to give, and two goats, and she became his wife.

"When we reached the Apingi village we saw three more Ishogos, and knew they too had been sold into slavery. This Apingi village was on the bank of a large river. After a few days the man who owned us sold us to another tribe called Aviia, living lower down on the banks of the river. A canoe took us there. Oh how frightened we became as we sailed in the little canoe! Happily we were sold together again, but the three other Ishogos did not go with us, so we had to bid them good-by. When night would come our new masters would leave people to watch us, and would put us in nchogo (a kind of stocks), and threatened us with death if we tried to escape.

"The Aviia man who owned us, wanting to marry a girl of another village, gave us to her father in order to get her, for he had bought us especially for this object. The Apingi had bought us for four large copper rings, and this man had bought us for eight—such as women wear round their ankles.

"We noticed, as we came down the river, that it got wider and deeper continually, and this filled our hearts with fear. We were resold again, and traveled in the forest, and afterward came to the river again. In this manner we were sold from tribe to tribe living down the river, taking larger canoes as we came down, till, one morning, when we came out into the sea, the canoe began to rock, and Mishoumbi and I almost died with fright.

"We then sailed along the coast till we came to the land of the Oroungous, who had bought us in the Ngalois country. The next morning they took us to some people looking like you. They were white men. They looked at us, they touched us, they felt us all over, and opened our mouths. Then the Oroungous sold us to them. We were so glad that Mishoumbi and I were sold together, for then we could talk together of Ishogo land—of our people. We knew that our country lay in the direction where the sun rose, and that we had come to the sea where the sun set. So every morning we would look toward the rising sun.

"A few days after we were resold to a white man, who sent us, before daylight, with many others, on board of a ship. It was quite dark. During the night we were put under the deck, and during the day we came out. There were on board many white men armed with guns and pistols, and the sight of them frightened us very much. All the men were kept together, and the women were apart, so I could only look at Mishoumbi, for we were not allowed to talk to any one.

"We could see that we were going away from where the sun rises, and going toward where it sets—going away, away, far away from the good Ishogo country, where we were born, and where our fathers of old were born. Fear was on the countenance of us all, for we knew not what was to become of us. We knew not if the white men were not to kill and eat us. We were afraid of the water, for land was nowhere to be seen.

"After two days and two nights we came in sight of an island. The land was as high as that of our Ishogo mountains. As we came near the land, canoes came alongside with white and black men on board, and took us all away, and landed us in the woods, where we slept, the people keeping guard over us. By-and-by some other white men came and bought us by sixes, eights, or tens. I parted with Mishoumbi, as I thought, forever; but no one dared to cry, for we were afraid of being killed on the spot.

"I was led, with seven others, to a plantation, and there I remained till I ran away, and it is there that I learned to speak Portuguese."

"How is it," said I, "that Mishoumbi and your three Ishogos friends are with you to-day?"

"Wait," said he, "and I will tell you. The island we came from is called St. Thomas.* The name of the master to whom I belonged was Silva; he was kind, and his plantation was by the sea. It had a great quantity of coffee-trees. All his slaves were free, after work, to walk to and fro. After being accustomed to the country, I began to visit round, and one day whom should I meet on a neighboring plantation but Mishoumbi—yes, Mishoumbi. She told me that our three Ishogos were living not far from her on another plantation, and from that time we saw each other very often. We would sometimes meet after our work was done, and talk of

* St. Thomas is about 250 miles from the coast, and is situated directly under the equator, almost in a parallel line with the Oroungou country.

Ishogo land, and look in the direction where the sun rises, knowing that the land we left was there. Often we said to ourselves, 'Only two days took us to this island; how pleasant it would be if we could go back, and live in the woods, and be free.'

"Then we began to talk all the time about running away, and very soon events occurred which helped us. My master wanted to teach me how to fish, and, after I had learned, I took a canoe every day and went out and fished. Of course I never went far from the land. After a while I became quite an expert canoeman. Dry seasons and rainy seasons passed away in that manner. One day I was ordered to make a big canoe from a tree that was in the forest, and, when the canoe was nearly finished, the idea came into my head of running away, and going again toward where the sun rises. When I told Mishoumbi of it, she said, 'Let us run away.' We swore to keep our plan a profound secret, and every evening, when we all met, we would say, 'Let us run away,' for the three Ishogos were to escape with us.

"The canoe was finished, and I was to take it to the beach in front of my master's house within a few days. In the mean time I had made paddles and prepared a sail of matting; and we collected food on the sly. One dark evening we all met in the woods, and, going down to the beach, launched the canoe, got into it, and paddled away from the island in the direction toward where the sun rises. The next morning we were far away, the land of St. Thomas appearing dimly in the horizon. The breeze bore us rapidly toward where the sun rises, but still we were afraid the people would chase us.

"Two days passed away, and no land came in sight.

Fear began to seize us, and we were sorry we had ran away. Four days more passed away, and still no land; we thought we should never see it again. Happily we had plenty of food, but the water began to get scarce. The fifth night a tornado blew and threatened to swamp us, but we collected a little water after the wind went down. The tornado was followed by a dead calm.

"While we were in all this trouble we spied a sail, and at first we thought it was in pursuit of us, which put us in great terror. Was it a St. Thomas vessel? If so, it would take us back, and our master would be hard upon us. But the vessel, after a while, changed its course; its sails grew dimmer and dimmer, and became lost to our sight. We continued to sail toward where the sun rises, hoping to find the land; but for a long time no land was to be seen, and at last we made up our minds that it was all over with us. But at last we saw the land! It did not look like the land of the Oroungous, and we were afraid, as we knew not where we were. But we had no food, no water, and we had to land or choose to die in our canoe."

We were much affected by the man's pathetic story, and told our new friends that they were free forever, as on this island there were no slaves. Here they would meet with some who, like themselves, had fled from where they came, though many more had perished in their attempt, while others have landed on the main land, and then were re-enslaved by the natives. We told them to go to sleep without fear. The next day they went to the old governor, who made them welcome to the little settlement of Freetown.

CHAPTER XXXII.

DEPARTURE FROM FERNANDO PO.—THE GULL.—HER CREW. —A TORNADO.—STARVATION.—CAPE ST. JOHN.—CORISCO. —GOOD-BY.

After a short visit to Fernando Po, I thought of going southward toward the equator to meet the *Roland*, but there was no vessel going there. Nothing was left for me to do but to buy a large boat, a kind of fishing-smack, which the governor of the island wished to sell. This boat was about ten tons burden. My great objection to it was that it had no deck; but, as there was no choice, I had to take it.

After buying the boat, the next thing was to get a crew. I went to friend Fasiko, and asked him to engage me a crew of four men, and sail down the coast with me. I immediately gave the name of Gull to our craft. The next morning Fasiko came with four strong, strapping fellows, all runaway slaves from the island of St. Thomas. They had before gone as sailors on board of vessels whose crews had been disabled by sickness. They said they were thoroughly good seamen—could splice a rope, go up the mast, knew how to cast an anchor, and steer a ship. They had kept their Portuguese names—Pedro, Antonio, Francisco, and Joannes. I named Fasiko captain, Pedro mate, Antonio and Joannes sailors, and Francisco cook, steward, and sailor into the bargain, if it became necessary. The boat was to be theirs when I

DEPARTURE FROM FERNANDO PO.

had done with it, and they would return to Fernando Po in it. I engaged them at the rate of ten dollars a month, with the promise of extra pay if they worked well. Discipline must be observed, and the night watches must be strictly kept.

I was afraid that the sailing qualities of the Gull were not very good, for her bow was not sharp, and she was too broad and too short. The first thing to be done was to put her in thorough trim for her voyage, and get provisions on board. So I bought from the natives sweet potatoes, yams, and a dozen fowls. I tried to get some sea-bread, but none could be obtained; but the good governor promised me some loaves of bread. I bought a brass kettle, an iron pot, some butter, two big pieces of salt pork, and two pieces of salt beef for my men, and a dozen boxes of sardines for myself. We also put on board a large quantity of fire-wood. Then I managed to get an old cask, which I sawed in two, and filled one half with sand. This one was to be our kitchen, and our fire was to be lighted on the sand. The other half was to be used as a kind of roof to the galley or kitchen, to protect the fire from the heavy rain and from the wind. This fire was to be kept up all through the voyage. My men being great smokers, I bought a good quantity of tobacco for them. I bought thick sailors' flannel shirts for each man. For myself, I had a thick water-proof cloak and several blankets. The uncomfortable point about the Gull was that there was no special place to sleep in.

As it would not have done to sail unarmed, I bought five trade-guns for my men, and, with my own, we had a formidable armament. I got papers from the governor for fear of being taken for a slave-dealer trading between the Coast and the island of St. Thomas.

Every thing being ready, we sailed. The morning was hot and sultry, and the very light breeze coming from the mountains of Fernando Po was hardly strong enough to move the boat. We sailed slowly past the island. The land-breeze gradually died away, and then the heat became intense. We had no awning, and I had not even an umbrella. There was, in fact, nothing to shelter me from the powerful rays of the sun, which seemed to pour down upon us with greater force than usual. When the land-breeze died away there was no sea-breeze coming to our help, and there we lay, a few miles from shore and from our point of departure, drifting slowly seaward. I had not bargained for this. The day passed away, and the sun began to sink beneath the horizon. Darkness followed, and with it came a certain relief from the terrible heat. During the day I kept three wet pocket-handkerchiefs in my hat to prevent me from being sunstruck.

Then came the rub. We must see what could be done to fix a place for sleeping. All that the sailors could do was to sleep on the bottom of the boat the best way they could. As for myself, I would sleep on the seat near the rudder. Before going to sleep I arranged for two watches. Fasiko, Pedro, and Antonio were to be in one; Francisco and Joannes were to belong, with myself, to the other. Happily, my Portuguese friends had learned English at Fernando Po, and could understand my directions pretty well. I said to them, "Boys, we are going to be good friends, but remember that there must be no sleeping when people keep watch, and" (pointing to a stick) "look out for the one who goes to sleep! for you know, boys, that this is the season of tornadoes, and that they sweep with terrible force across the sea, and should we be caught sleeping by the wind we should all be lost. I won't sleep when my turn for the watch comes," I added, in a laughing tone. "You may use the stick also on me if you catch me sleeping." Each watch was to last four hours—from eight to twelve P.M., from twelve to four, and from four to eight o'clock A.M. During the day, those who felt like sleeping could do so. Those whose watch lasted from eight P.M. to midnight were to sleep from six o'clock to eight.

During the whole of the night there was not a breath of wind. The sky was clear, and the stars shone beautifully. Toward four o'clock in the morning a light land-breeze began to be felt, and we commenced to make headway. The first twenty-four hours we had made very little progress from our starting-point, but I had great hopes that we should fare better the second day. But the second day was not a bit more favorable than the first, for we had neither land nor sea breeze. The way to navigate on this part of the coast is to take advantage in the morning of the land-breeze, and tack seaward, and in the afternoon, with the sea-breeze, to change the tack and make for the shore. The land-breeze would take us away from the coast almost in a straight line, while with the sea-tack we would approach the coast in a southeast direction; but thus far we had had a good deal more land than sea breeze, and were not successful in approaching the island. The farther we were from land the stronger became the current, which seemed to run somewhat from the southeast.

We were getting in a bad way. Four days had elapsed since we sailed from Fernando Po, and we were still in sight of the island, though far from it. It is true, I had ten days' provisions on board; but, if things went at this rate, we ran the risk of being twenty days on our voyage. I began to feel really anxious, though I did not want to show my feelings to the crew. I was thinking seriously of shortening our food allowance. Happily, we had two casks of water on board, and had plenty of it yet. The days were so hot that I did not know really what to do with myself, and I suffered very much from the glare of the sun. Toward nine o'clock on the evening of the fourth day out, the sky toward the land became dark and threatening, and it looked very much as if a storm was coming. After a while lurid flashes of lightning were seen. The distant mutterings of thunder could be heard, and these were getting nearer and nearer. I kept a sharp lookout on the horizon, and made every thing ready, so that the sails might be hauled down at the first glimpse of a tornado.

At length the thunder began to peal with tremendous force, and the rain to pour down in torrents. The claps of thunder were terrific. The storm lasted about four hours, and after it came a dead calm. Of course we were drenched to the very bone. The only thing to be done was to leave our clothes to dry upon us. The next morning, the fifth day after our departure, the sun, as usual, rose brightly, but there was hardly a breath of wind. As the storm had come directly from the land, it had blown us away from the coast, and, looking in the direction of the land, I saw that the bold outlines of the Peak of Fernando were lost to our sight.

The situation would certainly become critical if it lasted much longer. There we were, out of sight of land, with no breeze, and seemingly in one of those long spells of calm, when there was nothing to counteract the force of the strong contrary currents.

"Boys," I said to my crew, "we have plenty of provisions yet; but, as you see, we have been unfortunate with the breeze. Suppose we do not eat so much now as we did before, so that for sure we may not get out of food." "We will do just as you say," they replied, cheerfully; "we will only eat half of what we ought till we see a fair prospect of reaching the land." "That is right, boys," said I. So we began our short allowance of food from that day.

Quite a change in the weather soon took place, but, I am sorry to say, not for the better. Night after night the storm would burst upon us with terrible thunder, lightning, and rain. In one respect, however, these storms were of benefit to us, as they enabled us to collect water in our sails, and to fill our casks. The days were still intensely hot.

I took advantage of every little breeze we had, but the current was so tremendous that the Gull seemed to lose all the benefit of the wind. I was steering southeast, that is, making for the Coast; and now *fourteen days* had passed away, and there was no land in sight, though the last two days we had had a steady, good breeze.

It occurred to me at length that the compass by which I steered might be out of order, though I did not see how this could be, as there was no iron round it, my guns being all forward. The following day, when the sun rose, I took bearings with the compass, and, making due allowance for the deviation according to the longitude, I saw that the instrument was correct. Either the strong currents had put us out of the way, or some of the sailors must have steered badly. So I steered the Gull directly for the land. I was getting weak, as for the last ten days we had eaten very little food, just enough to keep us from starvation. I did not like the looks of an enormous shark that had been following us for three days. At night I could see its wake by the phosphorescent light it left behind it as it swam. He would come and almost touch the rudder. I shuddered at the thought of falling into the water, or of being upset by a tornado.

We all gradually became very weak. Were we to die of hunger at sea? It looked very much as if we were, as there was no more food left on board; happily we still had water to sustain us.

Seventeen days had passed since we left Fernando Po. That night the sky was clear, and the stars shone beautifully. The men were lying at the bottom of the boat, prostrated by heat and want of food. I was steering, for I did not dare to give the care of the rudder to any one. I wanted to make sure that the Gull was going right according to the compass. I had no strength left, as for two days I had taken no food except four little sardines, and my weak arm had all it could do to guide our boat. The wind was fair, and I was making right in the direction of the land. Shall we see it or not? As I looked toward the stars, I raised a silent prayer to God. The moon rose, and by its dim light I looked with sorrow on the care-worn, emaciated faces of my five faithful men, who had not even uttered a word of grumbling since we left. The night passed away, and the next morning, just as the sun was rising, I happened to look eastward. What do I see? "Land! land! boys," I shouted; "there is the land; look at it!" They all sprang to their feet to gaze at the blessed sight. It was Cape St. John. Joy succeeded sorrow. God had been with us, and had looked down upon the little Gull and its crew.

Toward noon we landed, so weakened by exposure and want of food that we could hardly walk. I tottered like a drunken man, I was so weak. The natives knew me, for, if you remember, we had been before at Cape St. John. The king of the village welcomed me and my men in a very friendly manner. Food was given us, and some chickens were presented to me by the kind African women. I forbade the men to eat much for a while, and that afternoon we had chicken broth. In the evening, also, we ate very little, for, if we had eaten heartily, no doubt it would have done us harm if it had not killed us.

That night I rested badly, for I was sore all over. The reaction had taken place, and all my strength seemed to have gone away with my anxiety. The next morning I was sick with fever, while a violent headache made me suffer terribly. The second day I felt better, and three days after my arrival at Cape St. John I sailed for the island of Corisco, thence down the Coast to meet the *Roland.*

This voyage from Fernando to Corisco had been fearful, and it required a long time for me to get over it.

In my preceding volumes you have been made acquainted with Corisco "the beautiful," and the countries of the main land; so I will leave you here, and promise to take you with me in my next volume into the country of the Dwarfs, which is situated far away in the interior mountains of Africa. These singular people are, no doubt, descendants of the same race described by the great historian Herodotus. They inhabit a country where, perhaps, some day, my dear Young Folks, one or two of you may follow me, and bring home news of what you have seen that will make the ears of your auditors tingle with wonder.

INTERESTING BOOKS

FOR THE YOUNG.

HARPER & BROTHERS *will send any of the following works by mail, postage prepaid, to any part of the United States, on receipt of the price.*

Du Chaillu's Apingi Kingdom. My Apingi Kingdom: with Life in the Great Sahara, and Sketches of the Chase of the Ostrich, Hyena, &c. By PAUL B. DU CHAILLU. Illustrated. 12mo, Cloth, $1 75.

Du Chaillu's Lost in the Jungle. Lost in the Jungle. By PAUL B. DU CHAILLU. Illustrated. 12mo, Cloth, $1 75.

Du Chaillu's Wild Life under the Equator. Wild Life under the Equator. By PAUL B. DU CHAILLU. Illustrated. 12mo, Cloth, $1 75.

Du Chaillu's Gorilla Country. Stories of the Gorilla Country. By PAUL B. DU CHAILLU. Illustrated. 12mo, Cloth, $1 75.

Adventures of a Young Naturalist. By LUCIEN BIART. Edited and Adapted by PARKER GILLMORE. With 117 Illustrations. 12mo, Cloth.

Puss-Cat Mew, and other New Fairy Stories for my Children. By E. H. KNATCHBULL-HUGESSEN. Illustrated. 12mo, Cloth.

Laboulaye's Fairy Book. Fairy Tales of all Nations. By EDOUARD LABOULAYE, Member of the Institute of France. Translated by MARY L. BOOTH. Elegantly Illustrated. 12mo, Cloth, $2 00; gilt, $2 50.

Macé's Fairy Tales. Home Fairy Tales (*Contes du Petit Château*). By JEAN MACÉ, Editor of the *Magasin d'Education*; Author of "The Story of a Mouthful of Bread," &c. Translated by MARY L. BOOTH. With Engravings. 12mo, Cloth, Beveled Edges, $1 75; gilt, $2 25.

Miss Mulock's Fairy Book. The best Popular Fairy Stories selected and rendered anew. Engravings. 16mo, Cloth, $1 50; gilt, $2 00.

Fairy Book Illustrated. Containing Twelve New Stories, expressly Translated for this Work. With 81 fine Engravings by ADAMS. 16mo, Cloth, $1 50; gilt, $2 00.

Bourne's London Merchants. Famous London Merchants. A Book for Boys. By H. R. FOX BOURNE. With Portrait of George Peabody and 24 Illustrations. 16mo, Cloth, $1 00.

Baker's Cast Up by the Sea. Cast Up by the Sea. A Book for Young People. By Sir SAMUEL BAKER, M.A., F.R.G.S., Author of the "Albert N'Yanza Great Basin of the Nile," "The Nile Tributaries of Abyssinia," &c. With numerous Illustrations. 12mo, Cloth, 75 cents.

Abbott's Romance of Spanish History. The Romance of Spanish History. By JOHN S. C. ABBOTT, Author of "The French Revolution," "The History of Napoleon Bonaparte," &c. With Illustrations. 12mo, Cloth, $2 00.

Abbott's Franconia Stories. Numerous Illustrations. Complete in 10 vols., 16mo, Cloth, 90 cents each. The volumes may be obtained separately; or complete, in neat case, $9 00:

Malleville.—Mary Bell.—Ellen Linn.—Wallace.—Beechnut.—Stuyvesant.—Agnes.—Mary Erskine.—Rodolphus.—Caroline.

Abbott's Little Learner Series. Harper's Picture-Books for the Nursery. Beautifully Illustrated. In 5 vols., 90 cents each. The volumes complete in themselves, and sold separately; or the Set complete, in case, for $4 50:

Learning to Talk.—Learning to Think.—Learning to Read.—Learning about Common Things.—Learning about Right and Wrong.

Abbott's Marco Paul's Voyages and Travels in the Pursuit of Knowledge. Beautifully Illustrated. Complete in 6 vols., 16mo, Cloth, 90 cents each. The Volumes may be obtained separately; or complete, in neat case, for $5 40:

In New York.—On the Erie Canal.—In the Forests of Maine.—In Vermont. —In Boston.—At the Springfield Armory.

Abbott's Stories of Rainbow and Lucky. Beautifully Illustrated. 5 vols., 16mo, Cloth, 90 cents per vol. The volumes may be obtained separately; or complete, in neat case, for $4 50:

Hardie.—Rainbow's Journey.—Selling Lucky.—Up the River.—The Three Pines.

Abbott's Illustrated Histories. Illustrated with numerous Engravings. 16mo, Cloth, $1 20 per vol. The volumes may be obtained separately; or the Set complete, in box, for $36 00:

Cyrus the Great.—Darius the Great.—Xerxes.—Alexander the Great.—Romulus.—Hannibal.—Pyrrhus.—Julius Cæsar.—Cleopatra.—Nero.—Alfred the Great.—William the Conqueror.—Richard I.—Richard II.—Richard III.—Mary Queen of Scots.—Queen Elizabeth.—Charles I.—Charles II.—Josephine.—Maria Antoinette.—Madame Roland.—Henry IV.—Margaret of Anjou.—Peter the Great.—Genghis Khan.—King Philip.—Hernando Cortez.—Joseph Bonaparte.—Queen Hortense.

Abbott's Young Christian Series. Very greatly Improved and Enlarged. Numerous Engravings. The volumes sold separately. Complete in 4 vols., 12mo, Cloth, $1 75 each:

The Young Christian.—The Corner-Stone.—The Way to do Good.—Hoaryhead and M'Donner.

Aikin's Evenings at Home; or, The Juvenile Budget Opened. By Dr. AIKIN and Mrs. BARBAULD. With 34 Engravings by ADAMS. 12mo, Cloth, $1 50.

A Child's History of England. By CHARLES DICKENS. 2 vols., 16mo, Cloth, $2 00.

A Child's History of the United States. By JOHN BONNER. 3 vols., 16mo, Cloth, $3 75.

A Child's History of Rome. By JOHN BONNER. With Illustrations. 2 vols., 16mo, Cloth, $2 50.

A Child's History of Greece. By JOHN BONNER. With Illustrations. 2 vols., 16mo, Cloth, $2 50.

Edgar's Boyhood of Great Men. With Illustrations. 16mo, Cloth, $1 20.

Edgar's Footprints of Famous Men. With Illustrations. 16mo, Cloth, $1 20.

Edgar's History for Boys; or, Annals of the Nations of Modern Europe. Illustrations. 16mo, Cloth, $1 20.

Edgar's Sea-Kings and Naval Heroes. A Book for Boys. Illustrated. 16mo, Cloth, $1 20.

Edgar's Wars of the Roses. Illustrations. 16mo, Cloth, $1 20.

Reid's Odd People. Being a Popular Description of Singular Races of Men. By Captain MAYNE REID. Illustrations. 16mo, Cloth, 75 cents.

Miss Mulock's Our Year. A Child's Book in Prose and Verse. Illustrated by CLARENCE DOBELL. 16mo, Cloth, Gilt Edges, $1 00.

Children's Picture-Books. Square 4to, about 300 pages each, beautifully printed on Tinted Paper, with many Illustrations by WEIR, STEINLE, OVERBECK, VEIT, SCHNORR, HARVEY, and others. Bound in Cloth, Gilt, $1 50 a volume; or the Series complete, in neat case, $7 50:

The Children's Bible Picture-Book.—The Children's Picture Fable-Book.—The Children's Picture-Book of Quadrupeds and other Mammalia.—The Children's Picture-Book of the Sagacity of Animals.—The Children's Picture-Book of Birds.

Harper's Boys' and Girls' Library. 32 Volumes. Engravings. 18mo, Cloth. Sold separately at 75 cents a volume:

Lives of the Apostles and Early Martyrs.—The Swiss Family Robinson, 2 vols. —Sunday Evenings, comprising Scripture Stories, 3 vols.—Mrs. Hofland's Son of a Genius.—Thatcher's Indian Traits, 2 vols.—Thatcher's Tales of the American Revolution.—Miss Eliza Robins's Tales from American History, 3 vols.—Mrs. Hofland's Young Crusoe; or, The Shipwrecked Boy.—Perils of the Sea.—Lives of Distinguished Females.—Mrs. Phelps's Caroline Westerley.—Mrs. Hughs's Ornaments Discovered.—The Clergyman's Orphan; the Infidel Reclaimed.—Uncle Philip's Natural History.—Uncle Philip's Evidences of Christianity.—Uncle Philip's History of Virginia.—Uncle Philip's American Forest.—Uncle Philip's History of New York, 2 vols.—Uncle Philip's Whale Fishery and the Polar Sea, 2 vols.—Uncle Philip's History of the Lost Colonies of Greenland.—Uncle Philip's History of Massachusetts, 2 vols. —Uncle Philip's History of New Hampshire, 2 vols.

Harper's Fireside Library: expressly adapted to the Domestic Circle, Sunday-Schools, &c. Cloth, 75 cents each:

Alden's Alice Gordon.—Alden's Lawyer's Daughter.—Alden's Young Schoolmistress.—Burdett's Arthur Martin.—The Dying Robin.—Ellen Herbert; or, Family Changes.—Mayhew's Good Genius that turned every thing into Gold. —William the Cottager.—Mayhew's Magic of Kindness.

Harper's Story Books. Narratives, Biographies, and Tales for the Young. By Jacob Abbott. With more than 1000 beautiful Engravings.

"Harper's Story Books" can be obtained complete in Twelve Volumes, each one containing Three Stories, at the price of $21 00; or in Thirty-six Thin Volumes, each containing One Story, at the price of $32 40. The volumes sold separately, the large ones at $1 75 each, the others at 90 cents each.

Volume I.—Bruno; Willie and the Mortgage; The Strait Gate.
" II.—The Little Louvre; Prank; Emma.
" III.—Virginia; Timboo and Joliba; Timboo and Fanny.
" IV.—The Harper Establishment; Franklin; The Studio.
" V.—The Story of Ancient History; The Story of English History; The Story of American History.
" VI.—John True; Elfred; The Museum.
" VII.—The Engineer; Rambles among the Alps; The Three Gold Dollars.
" VIII.—The Gibraltar Gallery; The Alcove; Dialogues.
" IX.—The Great Elm; Aunt Margaret; Vernon.
" X.—Carl and Jocko; Lapstone; Orkney the Peacemaker.
" XI.—Judge Justin; Minigo; Jasper.
" XII.—Congo; Viola; Little Paul.

Some of the Story Books are written particularly for Girls, and some for Boys; and the different volumes are adapted to various ages, so that the Series forms a complete Library of Story Books for Children of the Family and the Sunday-School.

Mayhew's Boyhood of Martin Luther; or, The Sufferings of the Little Beggar-Boy who afterward became the Great German Reformer. Beautifully Illustrated. 16mo, Cloth, $1 25.

Mayhew's Peasant-Boy Philosopher. The Story of the Peasant-Boy Philosopher; or, "A Child Gathering Pebbles on the Sea-Shore." (Founded on the Early Life of Ferguson, the Shepherd-Boy Astronomer, and intended to show how a Poor Lad became acquainted with the Principles of Natural Science.) Illustrations. 16mo, Cloth, $1 25.

Mayhew's Wonders of Science; or, Young Humphrey Davy (the Cornish Apothecary's Boy, who taught himself Natural Philosophy, and eventually became President of the Royal Society). The Life of a Wonderful Boy written for Boys. Illustrations. 16mo, Cloth, $1 25.

Mayhew's Young Benjamin Franklin; or, The Right Road through Life. A Story to show how Young Benjamin Learned the Principles which Raised him from a Printer's Boy to the First Embassador of the American Republic. A Boy's Book on a Boy's own Subject. With Illustrations by John Gilbert. 16mo, Cloth, $1 25.

Folks and Fairies. Stories for Little Children. By Lucy Randall Comfort. Illustrated. Square 4to, Cloth, $1 00.

Mrs. Mortimer's Reading without Tears; or, A Pleasant Mode of Learning to Read. Beautifully Illustrated. Small 4to, Cloth, 75 cents.

Mrs. Mortimer's Reading without Tears, Part II. Beautifully Illustrated. Small 4to, Cloth, $1 25.

Mrs. Mortimer's Lines Left Out; or, Some of the Histories left out in "Line upon Line." The First Part relates Events in the Times of the Patriarchs and the Judges. With Illustrations. 16mo, Cloth, 75 cents.

Mrs. Mortimer's More about Jesus. With Illustrations and a Map. 16mo, Cloth, 75 cents.

Mrs. Mortimer's Streaks of Light; or, Fifty-two Facts from the Bible for Fifty-two Sundays of the Year. Illustrations. 16mo, Cloth, Gilt, 75 cts.

Harry's Ladder to Learning. With 250 Illustrations. Square 4to, Cloth, 75 cents.

Harry's Summer in Ashcroft. Illustrations. Square 4to, Cloth, 75 cents.

Kingston's Fred Markham in Russia; or, The Boy Travellers in the Land of the Czar. By W. H. G. KINGSTON. Profusely and elegantly Illustrated. Small 4to, Cloth, Gilt, 75 cents.

The Adventures of Reuben Davidger, Seventeen Years and Four Months Captive among the Dyaks of Borneo. By JAMES GREENWOOD. With Engravings, 8vo, Cloth, $1 75.

Wild Sports of the World: A Book of Natural History and Adventure. By JAMES GREENWOOD, Author of "The True History of a Little Ragamuffin," "The Seven Curses of London," &c. With 147 Illustrations. Crown 8vo, Cloth, $2 50.

Self-Made Men. By CHARLES C. B. SEYMOUR. Many Portraits. 12mo, 588 pages, Cloth, $1 75.

Smiles's Self-Help: with Illustrations of Character and Conduct. By SAMUEL SMILES. 12mo, Cloth, $1 25.

Thackeray's Rose and the Ring; or, The History of Prince Giglio and Prince Bulbo. A Fireside Pantomime for Great and Small Children. By Mr. M. A. TITMARSH. Numerous Illustrations. Small 4to, Cloth, $1 00.

Wood's Homes without Hands: Being a Description of the Habitations of Animals, classed according to their Principle of Construction. By J. G. WOOD, M.A., F.L.S., Author of "Illustrated Natural History." With about 140 Illustrations, engraved on Wood by G. PEARSON, from Original Designs made by F. W. KEYL and E. A. SMITH, under the Author's Superintendence. 8vo, Cloth, Beveled, $4 50.

A French Country Family. Translated by the Author of "John Halifax" from the French of Madame DE WITT, *neé* GUIZOT. Illustrations. 12mo, Cloth, $1 50.

Nineteen Beautiful Years; or, Sketches of a Girl's Life. Written by her Sister. With an Introduction by Rev. R. S. FOSTER, D.D. 16mo, Cloth, $1 00.

Hooker's Child's Book of Nature. The Child's Book of Nature, for the Use of Families and Schools: intended to aid Mothers and Teachers in Training Children in the Observation of Nature. In Three Parts. Part I. Plants. Part II. Animals. Part III. Air, Water, Heat, Light, &c. By WORTHINGTON HOOKER, M.D. Engravings. The Three Parts complete in One Volume, Small 4to, Cloth, $2 00; or separately, 90 cents each.

Macé's History of a Mouthful of Bread, and its Effect on the Organization of Men and Animals. 12mo, Cloth, $1 75.

Macé's Servants of the Stomach. The Servants of the Stomach. By JEAN MACÉ, Author of "The History of a Mouthful of Bread," "Home Fairy Tales," &c., &c. Reprinted from the London Edition, Revised and Corrected. 12mo, Cloth, $1 75.

Miss Warner's Three Little Spades. Illustrations. 16mo, Cloth, $1 00.

www.ingramcontent.com/pod-product-compliance
Lightning Source LLC
LaVergne TN
LVHW010245110826
845151LV00004B/1396
* 9 7 8 1 4 2 5 5 2 3 2 1 3 *